No On
Are Remembered

Allan Horne

To

JANE

MY DOG IS MENTAL

XXX

MAMMOTH
MOUNTAIN
BOOKS

Published in 2019 by Mammoth Mountain Books

Copyright © Allan Horne 2019

Allan Horne has asserted his right to be identified as the author of
this Work in accordance with the Copyright, Designs
and Patents Act 1988

ISBN Paperback: 978-1-9162381-0-7
Ebook: 978-1-9162381-1-4

A CIP catalogue copy of this book can be found
in the British Library.

Published with the help of Indie Authors World
www.indieauthorsworld.com

IndieAuthors
World

Dedication

I dedicate this book to Ian - the older brother I looked up to each day; the brother who let me run with him since I was a kid; the brother who showed me the amazing world beyond our garden gate.

He was the brother who laughed with me, cried with me, sang with me, and fought with me, all through our lives. The brother who had my back from birth, and the one who was always there to get me out of the trouble I usually seemed to find myself in.

Also to my dad, who taught me right from wrong. The dad who worked his ass off to make sure he provided a better life for his kids, and the one who made sure we travelled the world as a family to experience life's people and cultures. As a merchant seaman, he passed on to me his love for travelling, his love of the world, and as I've recently discovered, he seems to have passed on his love of writing.

There is not a grave dug deep enough or dark enough that could stop either man's light from still shining through.

And finally, to my mum, who is Larkhall born and bred. If ever I thought Ian had my back in life, then it was nothing compared to this amazing lady. She would back her weans to the moon and back - although, of course, her weans did nothing wrong! Hers were good weans! She loves her town, loves her family, and loves a blether; by God, my mum loves a blether. And at 81 she is still as fit as a fiddle and sharp as a tack.

Without these three people in my life, I would not be the person I am.

I love you all.

Acknowledgements

At first when writing this book, it was my little secret. I am a self-employed plumber and one of my rooms in the house has been converted into my office. I would often sit there alone at night, unable to sleep. Initially, I started writing what to most people would look like a diary of the previous year's events. Then I started putting it all in sequence.

I am not joking when I say you would struggle to even find a Christmas card I had written previously, so I honestly have no idea where this writing came from. But for some strange reason it seemed to help me deal with things at that stage in my life. Escapism for want of a better word.

Before I knew it, I had been secretly writing for nearly a year and had in my possession what appeared to be a rough copy of a book. At that stage, I had not told a single person and was unsure about showing anyone what I had written. It was a personal journey, so I was not sure how people would react after reading it.

Eventually I plucked up the courage to show a copy to my wife Mhairi, to my brother's wife Jean, my cousin John Brown, my mate Andy Rankin, and the two Bullet Express owners Gary Smith and David McCutcheon.

Jean and Mhairi at first wouldn't, or couldn't, read it. They had both obviously been closely involved in the journey and their emotions were still a bit raw.

John, Andy, Gary, and David were soon on the phone, though, urging me to get it published.

I sat with it for months, going over it, changing bits here and adding bits there. Before I knew it, another year passed and I had done nothing. Every now and then I would be speaking to someone and mention I had written it, and people would ask to read it; sometimes I would even ask them to read it and let me know what they thought. Every one said the same thing, that I should send it away to be edited and published.

But time and life were moving on so quickly. I was involved with Ian's son Sandy in his Mini-Moto GP motorbike racing, and I was trying to deal with my own family, my personal issues with grief, and with everything else that such loss brings to the table.

So I put the book away and decided it was never going to be published.

The turning point, however, was year four. Sandy and his motorbiking were taking a different direction and I suddenly found myself with plenty of time on my hands and in need of something to focus on again. Sandy had taken me on his motorbike journey as far as he could, and on a sunny day at Silverstone Racetrack I finally felt I had a reason to finish this book and get it published.

I would like to give Sandy a great big thank you. For over four years he took me on an incredible journey with his motorbiking and, without him even realising it, he played a massive part in helping me through a difficult time. Thank you to my mate Andy Rankin who joined us on our motorbike journey, and without doubt played a major part in Sandy's life for the past four or five years and in my own life the past thirty years.

Thank you to Carmino Martucci and all the mums and dads who tirelessly drive up and down the country week in, week out, getting their kids on track, and to all who helped us over the past few years in racing. To Alan Lord at British Mini-Bike Championship, Crispin Vitoria at Cool Fab Racing Championships, and Alan McIntosh in the Scottish Mini-Bike Championship, and all the Scottish racing mums and dads for reaching out and helping both Sandy and me in a sport I knew nothing about but now have so much admiration for. You guys know who you are.

To Gary Smith and David McCutcheon - good friends of Ian's and owners of Bullet Express - for all the help they gave Ian, me, and Sandy at a difficult time, and all the support during the Land's End to John o' Groats cycle challenge with drivers Joe & Bobby.

Thank you to David Moulsdale from Optical Express for providing medical advice and different medical options.

To my cousin John Brown and close friends for trying to keep me sane through the years; that includes Gordon Hay, Alan Hay, David Forrest, Derrick Jones, Darren Richardson, Sandy Waddell, Stuart and Sara Gilmour, Kevin Melia, Elaine Beattie, Sheila Pacifico, and Carol Thomson.

Thank you to my own family - Mhairi, Alexandra, and Sacha - for walking alongside me at times when it would have been so much easier to take a different path.

And to Ian's family - his wife Jean, sons Dillon and Sandy, and his little princess Sara. Without looking for it, I am sure we are all closer as a family than we would have ever been. And by writing this book I really hope in even a small way it keeps Ian's memory with us for the rest of our lives. No-one dies if they are remembered.

A final thanks to all the medical staff at Ward 16 in Monklands Hospital and throughout the NHS who go out their way day in, day out, to make lives better for patients and their families. There were many tears shed in Ward 16 but there were also many, many laughs along the way. And we will always be grateful to Maggie's at Monklands Hospital for a stunning wedding day.

When I did finally feel I had a complete story to tell and eventually plucked up the courage to show a publisher, I came across Indie Authors World - a self-publishing company from Bishopbriggs in Glasgow, run by Kim and Sinclair Macleod.

Kim Macleod had written a moving true story of their own family's tragedy in losing their 12-year-old son Calum to meningitis. Her book, From Heartbreak to Happiness, really touched me and played a massive part in me choosing Indie Authors World to help self-publish my story.

At that point, I was told I had written a manuscript, but they felt confident they could help me turn it into a book. If truth be known, I never even knew what a manuscript was.

Kim decided Christine McPherson would be the best person to help me edit the manuscript. And over the next few months I enjoyed working with Christine and looked forward to having each chapter edited then sent back for me to go through and change things here and there.

When it was finally complete, I felt happy in a way, but sad that my time working with Christine was over. It was a great experience, and we had a good laugh near the end when she confessed something to me. (Let's just say, we don't follow the same football team!)

Kim and Sinclair have set up Calum's Legacy, which is a publishing project to help 16 to 25-year-olds become authors in their own right.

So, thank you, guys at Indie Authors World, and I wish you every success in the future with Calum's Legacy. I really hope it goes from strength to strength, and finally thanks to Kim Mcfarlane for turning what was only an idea in my head into a design and then creating it into a great illustration for the cover of my book.

If I have missed anyone out, please, please, please accept my apologies.

You can conact Allan at

allan@ahorneauthor.co.uk

https://www.facebook.com/AHorneAuthor/

Introduction

My first memory of Ian was him lying in a bath tub in front of a gas fire in my family home in the Birkenshaw area of Larkhall. Ian was just over three years older than me, and at that time I had to wait for him getting washed first before jumping into the water after him. It's bizarre to think of it now, but that was just how it was in those days.

We lived in a two-bedroom council house where Ian and I shared a room for over twenty years. The only thing that separated our beds was a chest of drawers, where at one point an old black and white tv sat, then a record player. Eventually we thought we had made it in the world when we had a stacked midi hifi unit with double tape deck.

We went to the same primary school, Craigbank Primary, and although primary one and two pupils were housed in a different part of the school from the older children, it didn't stop me from going round to see Ian at playtimes and lunchtimes where he would let me join in a game of football or other games with him and his pals.

By the time I got to Larkhall Academy, Ian was already going into 4th year and I can remember the "So you are Ian Horne's brother" comments from some of the teachers. Ian had a great knack of being able to pass exams while managing to bunk off school at times without getting caught. I clearly remember many occasions hiding in our garden shed waiting until Mum and Dad went to work, then we would just go back into the house and watch TV.

Over the years Ian and I spent many hours down the woods playing on rope swings or climbing trees, looking for birds' nests, fishing, shooting, or playing football. And he even introduced me to my first taste of alcohol when I was probably as young as twelve years old.

Ian was very intelligent and found schoolwork easy, and although he had regular run-ins with school authority, he managed to pass all his exams with good grades. In saying that, I think the school staff were happy when they heard there was no way he was staying on after his 16th birthday.

I, on the other hand, struggled at school, although perhaps if I'd applied myself differently I would have done much better. I followed the same path as Ian and got out of school as soon as possible – the only difference was I left with virtually no qualifications.

My brother and I had a great love of football, and I clearly remember Ian taking me to my first Glasgow Rangers match when Jock Wallace was manager in the 80s, and we enjoyed a 3-0 victory at home to St Mirren. Over the years, we travelled all over Europe together to watch games, and on one occasion we even borrowed a mate's mum's car to go to a football match. We just didn't mention to her that the match was in Bochum Germany!

After school we both gained apprenticeships - Ian as an electronics engineer and me as a plumber. By the time my training was finished, Ian had decided that working on the North Sea oil rigs was the way forward and had managed to get offshore employment with Shell UK. He convinced me to do my safety training and come out to work as a pipe-fitter on the rigs, where he had been promoted to Electronics Foreman. So offshore I went, and we worked together on different rigs for the next three or four years.

Ian then decided to come home from the North Sea and get into the electronics business, and soon after, I headed home and found a job with a local plumbing firm.

A few years passed and then we followed similar paths again, with Ian starting his own electronics company and me following with my own plumbing business. As the two companies grew, Ian and I both bought houses, got married, and started our own families. Ian had his son Dillon with his first wife, followed by Sara and Sandy with his second wife, Jean. My wife Mhairi and I have two girls, Alexandra and Sacha.

Ian eventually decided to get out of the electronics business a few years back, and enjoyed a more chilled approach to life where he went back to his love of fishing and shooting. He helped out as a fishing ghillie up near Fort William for a few months every year, which also involved taking clients out shooting. He loved his work up there, and although he still did occasional projects for electronics companies just to keep his hand in, I noticed a huge difference in the way he approached life at that time.

I hope the story I have shared can keep Ian's memory alive and in some way leave a small footprint in this world long after we leave this place. While I have no doubt that it will strike a chord with others facing similar situations, I hope that the laughter we shared at times shines through the sadness.

Silverstone racetrack, England

It's the 22nd of July, 2017, and I'm standing in the viewing gallery at the Stowe Circuit at Silverstone Racetrack in England, watching for a 12-year-old boy coming round the track on a Honda CRV 400cc racing motorbike.

Then I spot him. Every kid looks the same until you see their helmets, then you know who they are. The 12-year-old boy is my nephew, wee Sandy.

There is no rider for a fair distance in front of him, and no-one chasing up behind him. He is riding the 400cc bike effortlessly – not the fastest, but hitting apex to apex in the way he was told to do. When he gets to the straight part of track in front of me, he tucks into the bike the way he has been shown, and opens the throttle right up. At the end of the straight, he looks at the markers and uses them to come down the gears for braking before hitting the right to left-hand chicane. He changes down the gears perfectly at each marker, gets into the chicane, and goes away with the throttle opened up again.

As I watch him do this over and over again, a tear comes to my eye. I wish Ian was here to witness this; I really wish my mate Andy Rankin was here to see it.

I am well aware that this could be Sandy's last ride on a racing motorbike, but as I watch him, I detect a maturity in

Sandy that I have rarely seen before. He is doing exactly what he has been told to do: 'Forget everyone else; it is not a race. Only you can control what you can do. Nothing you do can affect others, so just concentrate on yourself. Close everything out apart from your own ride, and just try your best.'

It hits me there and then that our recovery and acceptance is nearly complete.

OK, let me explain...

Part One

1

'Never apologise for trusting your intuition, your brain can play tricks on you, your heart can make you blind, but very seldom is your gut feeling wrong.'

Rachel Wolchin, *author*

A phone call from my elderly mother on a cold autumn evening changed my life completely… and forever.

As a lifelong Glasgow Rangers fan, I'd gone with my friend, Andy Rankin, to Dumfries to watch our team play Queen of the South in a Challenge Cup match. We'd been friends for almost 30 years, since my older brother, Ian, first introduced us, and we often travelled to matches together.

Rangers had been demoted to the third tier of Scottish football, due to financial irregularities within the club, and were a far cry from the team we had supported for so long. Through the years, we had travelled all over Europe to support them, with great games to remember in such places as Barcelona, Munich, Turin, Moscow, Istanbul and Monaco. We were in Marseille the night Rangers were just one goal away from being the first British club to make the Champions League final in 1993 (one of the eight Champions League stars even represents our club), and we were at every match on the famous European run to the UEFA Cup Final in Manchester in 2008.

But that night – September 17, 2013 – we were in rather different surroundings, cheering them on at Palmerston Park in the Scottish Borders.

Just after half time, I took a call on my mobile phone from my mother, to let me know that my brother had been admitted to our local hospital, Wishaw General, with a stomach complaint.

A few weeks previously, Ian had told me he'd been sick while away on a business trip to Birmingham. On that occasion, he'd been treated in his hotel room by a doctor who suggested food poisoning. But it turned out to be so bad that Ian missed his friend's wedding, and was gutted that he'd been so ill that he hadn't even been able to speak to the guy in person to let him know.

The minute I switched the phone off to my mum that night, I just knew something wasn't right. Ian and I have always been as close as possibly two brothers could be. He and our dad had always been my heroes, bringing me up to enjoy life but never take it for granted, to grasp every opportunity, and to try to succeed in everything I do. Anyone who knows me will know that's exactly how I live my life, and I try to install the same principles in my own kids.

After mum's phone call, the game became irrelevant, and halfway through the second half I asked Andy if we could find a nearby pub where I could try and get in touch with Ian in the hospital.

When I got through to him, Ian assured me it was probably just food poisoning, but he had a feeling it might be some sort of hernia or appendix problem. As usual, he told me not to worry and that he would be out soon enough.

I don't really believe in telepathy, but I have spent more minutes and days with Ian than anyone else, and I know he does not do hospitals. Until that point, I had never known him to be ill, far less be admitted to hospital.

For some strange reason, the word cancer kept going through my head. I have no idea why I thought this, and I was actually quite annoyed at myself for even thinking it, but for some reason I felt things were bad. I just knew it. Sitting in a pub in Dumfries that night with my good friend Andy, I just knew that my brother and my hero had cancer. I didn't need to wait for doctors to tell me; my gut feeling was telling me, and I just knew.

2

*'More information is always better than less. When people
know the reason things are happening, even if it's bad
news, they can adjust the expectations and react accordingly.
Keeping people in the dark only serves to
stir negative emotions.'*

Simon Sinek, *motivational speaker*

The next few weeks were a bit surreal. I had noticed at my mum's 75th birthday party in the July that Ian had got a bit fatter. His face was puffy, and his belly was big. In fact, I'd been winding him up about his beer belly, but he blamed it on his bad diet.

For about a year, Ian had been taking his seven-year-old son, Sandy, to take part in go-karting at venues all over England. In Scotland, unfortunately, you are not allowed to race karts until you are aged eight. So, every weekend, Ian and Sandy would be away karting somewhere in England, eating convenience food like Pot Noodles, boil in the bag meals, crisps, chocolate, and beer. Ian had told me he would drink a case of beer over most weekends, and invariably felt awful from Monday to Thursday but would then follow the same routine the next weekend.

I have a picture of Ian at Mum's 75th birthday, looking not so much big, but puffier than I was used to seeing him. However, at the time, we had both just laughed it off.

The day after Mum's phone call, I went to the hospital to visit Ian. When the two of us were on our own, he admitted he was a little bit concerned about his condition. He had been to his local GP a few weeks before to show him his swollen stomach, and the GP had mentioned the usual things – non-bowel movement; trapped wind; fluid build-up caused by his bad diet – but said to contact him again if things got worse. When Ian did contact him after a couple of weeks, he was told to go straight to Wishaw General Hospital.

At this point, he probably looked like a seven or eight-month pregnant woman.

On arrival at hospital, he was told to immediately fast so that he could get an endoscopy and colonoscopy procedure carried out. Unfortunately, the procedure was cancelled the first day and had to be done the following day, which meant him fasting for two days. Then, after the endoscopy, Ian struggled to eat anything as his throat felt scratched and sore and he often felt nauseous. This obviously then affected his mood and he felt fatigued and his weight began to plummet.

All through this, I kept telling him to just keep trying to eat as much as he could to try and build his strength back up. To make matters worse, we waited nearly a week to get the results back from the tests only to be told that they were inconclusive, so more tests followed. This time, Ian was to have his first CT scan, and again he was asked to fast beforehand. It didn't prove to be a problem for him, because he hardly eaten a thing in over a week, but then he was asked to drink something which I can only describe as the most powerful laxative known to man. Within an hour, basically every bit of fluid had been flushed out of his body.

I am sure I speak for many patients' families here when I say that during the time when you don't know what is wrong, every second seems an hour, every hour a day, and every day a month. You live life in a bubble. You just want to know, good or bad. You start to dislike the doctors, the nurses, even other people talking about people they know in hospital. Looking back, the doctors and nurses were great with Ian, but at that particular time I just disliked and had no trust or confidence in anything associated with the NHS.

Ian drank Gastrografin, which is the dye used to help with the CT scan. Again, we had to wait. Again, the tests came back inconclusive.

How could all these tests keep coming back with no conclusion about what was wrong with Ian. We kept asking why, but no-one could give us an answer.

It was decided that a biopsy would be taken from Ian's stomach, so he was again asked to fast for a full day. The next day he was transported to Hairmyres Hospital fifteen miles away in the town of East Kilbride… only for the procedure to be cancelled at the last minute by the radiographer, and Ian sent back to Wishaw General.

Ian had spoken to his doctor and been told that the radiographer was concerned about taking a biopsy in case it caused more harm to Ian's condition. But by this time, his stomach had grown dramatically, his weight had dropped about 30lbs, and he looked gravely ill.

Frustrated and worried, Ian called me to say that the doctor thought he had a type of tumour which only two hospitals in the whole of the UK deal with – Dundee and Basingstoke. He also revealed that it was a large tumour, but they could not be 100% sure what it was until more tests were carried out.

Ian was now struggling to breathe. The build-up of fluid in his stomach was pressing on his diaphragm, and his lungs were not fully opening and closing. He kept saying he was convinced his lungs were filling up with fluid, and he was finding it hard to breathe and even talk.

I deliberately went into the hospital the next morning to see the doctor doing his rounds. I told him that Ian needed a fluid drip fitted to build up his strength, along with a lung drain. He seemed to be drowning with his lungs filling up with fluid. *What is wrong with these guys?* I kept asking myself. However, I was assured it would get fixed later that day.

I have a few nurse friends and a surgeon I go hillwalking with, so I contacted them, explained the situation, and let them know about the tumour and the doctor mentioning Dundee & Basingstoke. One got back to me pretty quickly with news I did not really want to hear.

Dundee and Basingstoke, I was told, both have surgeons who deal with a rare cancer condition called Pseudomyxomo Peritonei. It is so rare that the chances of catching it, or having it, are about one million-to-one. *Surely Ian can't have this?* I thought. *It's a one-in-a-million chance, could Ian be that unlucky?*

In the meantime, Ian had been told he was going to be taken back to Hairmyres Hospital for a biopsy the next day, so it meant another fast. The situation was becoming absolutely cruel and unbelievable!

The following morning, I went straight up to Ian's bed and waited until the doctor came for his daily rounds. This time, we just asked him outright what he personally thought was wrong. He dropped the bombshell by saying the radiographer thought it might be a condition known as Pseudomyxomo Peritonei. From my conversations with my medical friends, I discovered that this rare condition is also known as 'Jelly Belly', which would explain Ian's swollen stomach.

My surgeon friend explained that if the diagnosis was confirmed, Ian would most likely be sent to Basingstoke in

Hampshire for intensive treatment, which would require him being in hospital there for five or six months to have a number of operations, follow-up treatment, and recovery. Along with some website links to look at, she also warned me that Ian's life would be completely different when he eventually returned to Scotland.

The information I found online made grim reading, and I admit I was petrified. Even worse, I had to go into the hospital and explain to my brother what I had been told and what was likely to be the next step.

As usual, Ian made a joke of the situation. 'Ok, basically I am going to be opened up, a few parts that I don't need taken out and thrown away, a wee hose down for a clean, and stitched back up. I can do that,' he said, then added, 'Are there any good nightclubs in Basingstoke, as it looks like we are moving there?'

The next step we took was to get in contact with David Moulsdale, who is one of Ian's business colleagues and a friend. David is the owner of Optical Express, a leading optical firm which also specialises in cosmetic surgery, so he has medical contacts throughout the world. As usual, David was not in the UK, but we managed to contact him in Tokyo, and he immediately got onto the case.

After going over everything, he decided that the Mayo Clinic in Arizona, USA, would be the best place to deal with Ian's condition, so several emails were passed back and forth. At one point I was talking to David in Tokyo, while he was live on the phone to Doctor Alan Bryce in Arizona, who specialises in this sort of cancer in the States. I was thinking this was absolutely bizarre.

According to his biography, Dr Bryce is the Medical Director of the Genomic Oncology Clinic at Mayo Clinic,

Arizona, where he 'utilizes whole genome sequencing of tumours to identify key driver mutations. This approach allows for precise targeting of a patient's tumour, leading to a greater chance of remission. Dr Bryce was present during the first Sugarbaker technique and is one of the top surgeons throughout the USA who uses this method.'

As a family, we were all in a bit of a spin at this stage. We'd gone from thinking Ian had a hernia or something non-threatening, then facing him being moved to Basingstoke in England, to now talking about flying him to Arizona in the US.

David Moulsdale is a lovely guy, and we all appreciated the effort and time he was putting into this Mayo Clinic option, but he had not seen the condition Ian was in by then, and I knew my brother was not fit to fly to America. He could hardly get into a wheelchair to get to the front door of the hospital, never mind jump in a taxi, get to an airport, and get a flight to the USA.

Nevertheless, I asked David to get up and see Ian as soon as he returned to Scotland, but in the meantime to do as much as he could to save my brother's life.

3

*'Either you give in, or you fight. That's all I know, being
where I'm from. You fight for what you want, or you give up.
I was not about to give up.'*

Allen Iverson, *US athlete*

The next day (Friday) was a bit of a blur as we were still
waiting on Ian going to Hairmyres for the biopsy,
which would then be sent to Basingstoke to confirm it was
Pseudomyxoma Peronei.

I asked the doctor about my brother's lung problem and he said
that when Ian returned from Hairmyres, he would get someone
down to check his lungs for fluid and possibly fit a drain.

Ian mentioned that as it was the local September holiday
weekend, his doctor was going to be off until the Monday or
Tuesday. But my brother assured me he would call me later to
let me know how things had gone with the biopsy, so I went
to work and tried to keep busy.

All day I waited; every time a customer rang, I hoped it was
Ian...but there was no word from him. I tried phoning his
mobile, but it just went to his voicemail. I called his partner,
Jean, but she said she had been in the same situation, waiting
to hear from him.

Eventually, about 6pm, Ian called to say that the radiographer had yet again refused to do a biopsy and he was being

sent back to Wishaw General. I could not believe what I was hearing.

When I took his call, I was still at a customer's house and could not show the hell I was in at that point. I sat on the back doorstep in a daze, trying to make some sense of the whole situation. My brother had 'walked' into Wishaw General Hospital with a stomach ache, and within about two weeks I had watched him drop around 2 stones in weight, drained of every ounce of fluid, been starved , fasted, had tubes put down his throat, up his ass, given blood test after blood test, and a CT Scan. And now a radiographer was refusing to carry out a biopsy to find out what was wrong with him.

I sat for a while, then I furiously started typing out an email to the doctor who had decided his holiday was more important than my brother's condition. I have never felt so helpless in my life, but I knew I had to do anything I could for my brother.

In my email, I wrote:

> *Good evening, Dr ***, hope you're having a nice night off,*
>> *Let me update you with my brother's condition!!!*
>> *Yet again my brother has fasted for a whole day to get this keyhole biopsy thing done. Every second seems like an hour for us, and every hour seems like a day!!!*
>> *And yet again here we are with Wishaw General refusing to do it and Hairmyres Hospital in East Kilbride refusing to even see Ian for the next day or two. What is it with you guys? Please give me your reason for refusing to do this today, and the reason why this is not being carried out, and no doubt another day fasting for Ian tomorrow!!! Are you guys trying to starve him to death quicker than the cancer?? Why are you constantly putting my brother through hell?*

I know Ian is in a bad way – Stevie Wonder could see that – but why, why, why do you guys never do what's needed when it IS needed? Last Thursday you were in the room and you could see Ian was struggling for breath, yet it wasn't until he nearly drowned that fluid was taken from his lung. A few days before, we mentioned about Ian struggling to eat and that he needed fluids. Yet again, you said you would get it sorted the next day, but it took 3 days!!!! Ian was dehydrated yet a drip was not inserted for 2 days...

I'm no nurse or doctor, but I have seen Ian WALK into hospital and being drained of every ounce of fluid and every ounce of energy!!! He has been to hell and back over the last 2 weeks, and so have we as his family...

He is now eating again and trying to build his strength up!!! Every day I take about 50 calls asking the same question... 'Why is it taking so long to diagnose the problem? Why won't they go in and have a look?' So I ask you, Dr ***, WHY? Someone somewhere grow a pair of balls and get in have a look and get out... I know in this day and age you have to jump through hoops not to hurt people's feelings in case of comebacks, but we are old-school... a spade is a spade. If you can tell by this email that I am a bit pissed off, then that is exactly the case... He is probably only a number and a patient to you, but he is my older brother, my mother's oldest son, a father of three, and a happy family guy.

If you are scared to go in, then please, as I said earlier, grow some... Ian has given you permission to get this done.

Ian is very intelligent. He will ask you the correct questions, and I am sure he will not want to upset anyone on the ward or anyone that is treating him, however please don't take kindness as a weakness and simply think you can get to Ian tomorrow, as that is what it is starting to look like.

I think it is a total disgrace the way you have treated my brother, especially mentally but also physically. Another day of fasting when he could be eating to build strength. And no doubt fast all over again tomorrow... (If you ever actually bother seeing him!

Allan Horne

I also sent a copy of the email to Ian, with the message:

'Sorry, Ian!!! I sent this to Doctor *** See u at 7 x'

I got a reply from Ian:

'Good, mate. I just flung the telly out the window. Thanks, Ian'

The doctor cancelled his time off and visited Ian on the Friday night, several hours after I'd sent the email. Ian let him know we wanted all his notes and scans sent to Dr. Bryce at the Mayo clinic in Arizona, as emails had already been exchanged between David Moulsdale, the Mayo Clinic, Ian, his partner Jean, and me.

He then immediately assigned a nurse to Ian and announced that he would be taken back to Hairmyres where the radiographer **WOULD** carry out the biopsy this time. Ian was also told that his lung would be seen to as soon as possible.

Finally, after weeks of toing and froing and delay after delay, the doctor was true to his word and Ian got his biopsy. He also put Ian's notes and scans onto a disk and personally delivered them to Jean's work, where she sent them straight to Dr Bryce in Mayo Clinic Arizona.

I spent the Saturday night with Ian in his hospital room. I had sneaked in a couple of cans of beer, cider, and sweetheart stout. Ian drank a little stout and I had the rest. Although the nurses did not know about the alcohol, they turned a blind eye to me being in his room after visiting time.

Ian kept complaining about fluid in his lungs and that he could not breathe, but he wanted to see outside, he wanted to feel the fresh air. Looking back, I honestly, hand on heart, believed he thought it was going to be his last chance to see outside.

Without giving it any real thought, I helped him into the wheelchair, pushed him onto the lift, and took him to the basement of Wishaw General. I had no idea where I was going, but as I was wheeling him along the corridor we both noticed we were on the morgue level. Ian joked, 'Not yet, Allan.'

When we got outside for fresh air, a few patients were at the door smoking. Ian being Ian said in a loud voice, 'Nothing like coming to the door of a hospital for fresh air. First thing you smell arriving and leaving this fucking place is smoke! Take me back to the morgue, bruv, the dead don't smoke.'

I wheeled him back to his room where we watched X-Factor. A few nurses came into the room for a look, as one of the finalists on the programme was a lad from Wishaw called Nicholas Macdonald. I was more concerned in case they noticed the cider behind the IV drip!

When I went home that night, I believed that wheeling Ian along the corridor of the morgue and to outside was likely to be the last thing I was ever going to do for him.

Next day, Ian had 2.5 litres of fluid drained from his lung. That's just a number to a lot of people, but if you think of the size of a 2-litre bottle of Coke and imagine one of those in your lung along with another quarter-bottle, it gives you an idea of the amount of fluid that had gathered there.

Basingstoke had been kept in touch and Ian's scans and blood results had all been sent down there, so we were patiently waiting on them getting back to us.

David Moulsdale had one of his guys on the case. In fact, he had been phoning Basingstoke and pretending to be me, which was confusing for Basingstoke as I had just been on the phone to them as well!

Dr Tom Cecil at Basingstoke was the doctor who was assigned to find out if Ian had Pseudomyxomo Peritonei. He had actually worked with Dr Paul Sugarbaker who had performed a tumour removal procedure now known as the Sugarbaker technique. So, if anyone was going to know what Ian had, my money was on Dr Tom Cecil in Basingstoke and Dr Bryce in Arizona, not anyone at Wishaw General or Hairmyres.

Everything seemed to go into overdrive after the email. I would love to think it was coincidence, but as time went on Ian mentioned a few times that he reckoned my intervention had probably saved his life.

I have a different theory and, whether true or completely inaccurate, what I am about to write is my theory.

The NHS only have enough beds and money to treat a certain amount of cancer patients. If I had not emailed Dr ***, Ian would have drowned the next day from the fluid build-up in his lungs and we would have received a call to say that it was fast and there was nothing could be done to save him. The NHS would then have had one less cancer patient to worry about. How would we have known any different? How many families get that exact call and openly accept it?

Ian was only 46 years old, and had enjoyed good general health up to that point. Five years earlier, my dad died of the same illness Ian had, and we just accepted the doctors' word when they said surgery was not an option. Dad's age was a concern, and we were told he had only had three to four weeks to live. We just accepted this and lived with his fate.

I believe somebody somewhere is playing God and decides who lives, depending on hospital space and money, and who dies…

Who are we to question it?

It costs thousands of pounds to treat cancer patients, and if there is no hope or doctors are just delaying the inevitable, in my opinion they will not treat you.

Anyway, that's just what I believe, and I am not looking for anyone to agree or disagree. It is only my personal opinion.

*

A few days later, we got news that took our path in another direction.

Basingstoke confirmed Ian **did not** have Pseudomyxomo Peritonei, and confirmed that he in fact had Burkett's Lymphoma.

For several weeks, even with the odds of one million-to-one, we honestly believed Ian had Pseudomyxomo Peritonei. Everything pointed to it and, although I would have loved to rattle the radiographer for misleading us, I can see why he might have thought it.

We had talked about renting a house in Basingstoke; we had consultants in the Mayo Clinic, USA, working on Ian's case; we had all the info in our heads about what we were preparing for. Then in one sentence that no longer mattered.

Burkett's Lymphoma was now the condition we had to focus on, and we were told before Googling everything that there was a cure and a great chance Ian was going to pull through.

Ian would now be moved from Wishaw General to Ward 16 at Monklands Hospital, which was to be his new home from home for the next nine months.

4

'Every day is a chance to change and begin again. Don't
focus on the failure of yesterday, but start today with positive
thoughts and expectations.'

Catherine Pulsifer, *author*

I must admit that as positive as we were, I was worried when I heard that Ian was going to be treated at Monklands Hospital, because we hadn't been happy with the treatment my dad received when he was a patient there. My dad was blind, and I can still remember visiting him at night and finding his wash basin still full of facial hair and cold water from his morning shave. On a few occasions, we had to ask for his dirty sheets to be changed, and we were unhappy that his window blinds were broken and lying on the ground, allowing anyone walking past to looking in the window.

But I will say this now: Monklands Hospital's Ward 16 is as good as any hospital ward I have ever seen or visited; the staff are a credit to the place; and the treatment Ian received there was as good as we could expect anywhere.

From the moment we arrived, the whole professional side kicked off. No longer were there lots of visitors; no children under 12 years, apart from his little princess, Sara, and his wee champ, Sandy; and the room was at a set temperature. Ian was only allowed a maximum of two visitors, and initially we had to wear gowns and gloves when seeing Ian. There were also no more after-hours visits with stout and cider, but we did manage to sneak in the odd beer for Ian and a few mates from time to time.

Ian's treatment started right away, with lots of steroids to start with and chemotherapy treatment almost immediately. I remember his legs swelling up due to the steroids, although his stomach began to reduce in size right away. He also had a room to himself to start with, which was perfect as it gave him some privacy while coming to terms with the treatment he was about to undertake.

When Ian got settled, he discussed everything with the new doctors and was given a run-down on his condition. He was told that the symptoms of Burkett Lymphoma often come on over just a few weeks, because the lymphoma cells are dividing so quickly. For the same reason, it is common for the lymphoma to be in several places by the time it is diagnosed.

Ian was told he would be more or less in hospital for the next four or five months, being given intensive chemotherapy sessions. The doctors explained that Burkett Lymphoma is best treated with and can often be cured by intensive chemotherapy.

*

Every year, during the spring and summer months, Ian would go up to Torlundy Estate just outside Fort William, to help his friend, John Veitch, as a ghillie at Camisky Lodge, and work the River Lochy. So, it was nice that one of the first visitors at Ian's new home-from-home was John.

Having travelled down from the Highlands, he presented Ian with a big picture of the River Lochy with Ben Nevis in the background. Ian loved the picture and got it put up on his wall in his room.

He had a lot of respect for John and had always loved his job up there fishing and stalking the river. He also loved climbing Ben Nevis. Both Ian and I have always been keen climbers and have enjoyed some great climbs on the Ben; we've climbed our two favourites – Tower Ridge and the Ledge Route –a good few times together, in both winter and summer. Anyone that knows the mountain will know that in the winter both are alpine-classed and extremely hard climbs to do.

In my view, one of the best things we did together was to climb Tower Ridge a few years ago in winter. By the time we topped it and got back down, we were completely done-in and had to stay at a hotel that night to recover, as we were in no position to make the three-hour drive back home.

Another of the early visitors to Monklands was David Moulsdale, who had concluded his business in the Far East and come straight up to see Ian.

After discussing all the scenarios, Ian, David, and Ian's partner Jean agreed that visiting the Mayo Clinic in the US was now out of the equation and that Monklands Hospital was going to be the best place for my brother's treatment.

So, Ian was now preparing to face seven to nine months of intensive chemotherapy and various other treatments in his quest to beat this horrible disease.

5

'Uncertainty does not make life's path easy. Sometimes you just have to take it all in, have a laugh, have a smile and when the opportunity presents itself be ready to take the gamble.'

Badair Nevada, *2011*

Immediately, the drugs and treatment seemed to be doing their job. Ian's stomach started to reduce in size, he started to eat again, and although his frame was very small, he started to look like Ian again. The downside of him feeling better, though, was he got moved out his room which he liked and into a ward with another three patients. His fellow 'inmates' seemed to change every other day. Ian was spending a long time in the hospital, while the others were just coming in for a few days, either to be diagnosed or because they'd suffered a relapse and needed a few days' treatment.

A few guys stood out to me. One patient across from Ian had just been told there was nothing they could do for him. He had been diagnosed as terminal and, as Ian put it, they were just giving him a bag of pills to go home with to probably keep the pain at bay, but no doubt he would be dead in a few weeks. I watched as the man's son came in and they started playing cards. The son was probably younger than me, and I wondered if his dad had told him about his condition yet.

It brought back memories of finding out that my own dad was terminally ill with cancer. I remember sitting in the conservatory in my house when Ian called me to let me know he had been to see Dad and been told there was nothing that could be done to save him. He was returning home with some very strong pain relief treatment to make his final weeks bearable. As I mentioned earlier, we just accepted the decision on the advice of the doctors, and my dad did pass away about three weeks later.

Everyone in Ian's ward seemed to be older than him. In all the time I went to visit, I never seemed to see any younger or middle-aged men, just older guys. One was a well-off and well-known owner of a chain of shops. Ian said that for such a successful man, he was the most pessimistic guy he had ever come across. To be fair, the guy was gravely ill and, from what I heard, he died shortly afterwards.

Ian was young, though, and he was taking this huge battle in his stride. Our mate Andy and I regularly took in pizza for him, and I enjoyed a few kebabs with him on a few occasions.

I remember one day I was working in Glasgow when Ian phoned and asked if there was any chance I could go to McDonalds and bring him in an ice cream McFlurry. For some reason, he seemed to have an addiction to that particular ice cream at that stage of his treatment. I just laughed and said, 'Yeah, give me half an hour.' I told my customer that I had to pop away to get some materials, but headed to the nearest McDonalds.

As I was heading to the hospital with two McFlurrys sitting on the passenger's seat, I was stopped by the police for speeding. Apologising to the officers, I explained about Ian and his condition, and where and why I was going. At this point I would love to say the police were reasonable and let me off with a warning, but no. They made me sit in the back of their police car and go over all my details, insurance, driving licence, registration, and then told me they wanted to do a 'routine' vehicle inspection. They eventually let me go after checking my works van for everything from bald tyres to illegal fuel. As I drove away, I must confess I muttered quite a few expletives at them.

By the time I finally reached Ward 16, the McFlurry was basically a milk shake, and Ian gave me a hard time about the time I had taken to bring it. Not to be outdone, he asked if I could pop down to the local McDonalds, near the hospital, and buy another one... and as it was now lunchtime, could I get him a Big Mac and chips as well!

Ian thought it was pretty amusing about me being stopped for speeding and receiving a fine and penalty points on my licence, but suggested that if I got stopped by the police in future, I should use his name and address and any points would be put on his licence. He reckoned it might be a while before he really needed his driving licence again!

Ian was getting stronger each day and all the signs were good, so were hopeful that everything was going to be okay. One night, he phoned and asked me to meet him at the main door of the hospital, and to bring a jacket and a can of Sweetheart stout. He said he was going a bit stir crazy and the beeps on the monitors were driving him mad.

His chemo session was due to finish at 5pm, so he asked the nurse if he could go for a walk to the canteen. Instead, he met me at the main door and said he wanted to go for a run in the car. He didn't care where or for how long; he just wanted away from the hospital and to be 'normal' for an hour or two.

Ian turned up wearing a pair of jogging pants, a pair of slippers, and a hoodie. Because of the weight he had lost, everything just looked huge on him.

We worked out that the nurses probably wouldn't notice he was gone until after visiting time at 8pm. So, we ended up going for an Indian meal in a restaurant near the hospital, where Ian just picked at his food. He asked the waiters if it was okay for him to open his can of stout, after explaining that he was 'on the run from Monklands Hospital'. They said it was no problem.

When we left there, we went to the bookmakers and I told Ian I was going to put money on some of the Champions League football ties. I was betting on Ajax from Amsterdam to beat Barcelona, and Celtic to lose at home to AC Milan. It was a double bet, but it was the only combination that would put Celtic out of the Champions League but also out of the Europa League as well, as it would see them finish last in the group. As Rangers fans, Celtic are our arch-rivals, and the double bet was giving us odds of 13/1.

Ian thought this idea was hilarious and wanted to go put the bet on himself. So, I gave him £20 and he went into the bookmakers with his slippers, jogging pants, and hoodie on. I was laughing my head off watching him, so proud that he was not allowing this terrible illness to get the better of him.

We left there and went to Go Outdoors – a shop that sells everything to do with the great outdoors. We headed straight to the climbing section, and I asked Ian if he would do another climb with me once he got out of hospital. 'Yeah,' he said. 'We will climb the Inaccessible Pinnacle on the Isle of Skye.'

The Inaccessible Pinnacle is part of the Cuillin Ridge on the Isle of Skye. It's classed as a Munro, which is the name given to all mountains in Scotland which are higher than 3000ft above sea level. What makes this one so special is that it is a rock face that has to be climbed with ropes, and eventually you have to abseil to get back off it. I had done it before and knew how challenging it could be, but I had never climbed it with Ian. We decided it would be a great goal to set him and a new experience after his treatment.

One quick look at our watches said it was time to take Ian back to his monitors, beeps, and dials, before the nurses realised he was missing. So, I dropped him off at the front door of the hospital and away he went as if he didn't have a care in the world, wearing clothes that were about two sizes too big for him.

I went home and watched the football. Ajax beat Barcelona and AC Milan beat Celtic that night, so Ian won £260. Happy days!

*

As the weeks passed, Ian was allowed home for a few days here and there, but each time seemed to catch an infection due to his immune system being all over the place... or non-existent.

One of the times he ended up in the High Dependency Unit back at Wishaw General Hospital. While he was there, he caught an infection in the pick line on his arm, which really annoyed him because he'd had no infection until he entered Wishaw. He complained that the hygiene standards there weren't as good as at Monklands Hospital, but when we went to visit him in Wishaw you would have thought we were about to deliver a child the way we had to dress to see him. I wasn't even allowed to touch him, and we had to stay one metre away from his bed the whole time!

That was when Ian was probably at his worst spell throughout his treatment, just before, during, and after Christmas. I went in to see him just before Christmas and reminded him of a time when we'd been caught in bad weather when climbing in the Glencoe mountains. We'd had to dig a snow hole, and spent a cold night on top of the mountain. Our shared joke was that his midget gem sweets saved my life, because I had eaten all my food and he kept winding me up that night that I was going to starve to death before we froze to death.

That night, I promised him I would get him out of hospital, and we would climb another mountain again. I suggested the Isle of Skye and the Inaccessible Pinnacle, which Ian had spoken about, but he said he would just be happy to get out and climb Tinto Hill – a small, local hill the pair of us used to climb as kids. 'Okay,' I agreed, 'that will be the first hill we climb when you get out.

When I got home that night, I put a post on Facebook trying to get across my positivity about the situation.
I posted:

> '2 years ago in one of the year's shortest days, me and my bruv Ian mistimed a climb on Curved Ridge Glencoe and had to dig a snow hole n spend the night up there. His midget gems saved my life... I won't be climbing with Ian this winter because of his illness, but mark my words now, by the time the longest day 2014 comes around I promise I'll have him up and over Inaccessible Pinnacle on Skye Ridge. Isle of Skye... Any climbing friends want to help, you are more than welcome to come along. Piece of piss, Ian.'

The post attracted a fair amount of replies from friends and climbers we had known over the years, and I just hoped when Ian got out that we would indeed be able to make the climb.

*

Throughout Ian's time in hospital, plenty of friends came to visit, particularly at the start of his illness. Unfortunately, a lot came along for a few visits at the start but as time went on, they just disappeared. What opened my eyes were the ones who came along and stayed all the way through Ian's treatment,

Graeme Easton was one of those guys. Ian knew him from an air rifle shooting club they had set up together, I got to know Graeme through my brother. I even found out a few things about Ian that I had not known before. It turns out that they both went on to shoot in the World Championships together, over four years in a row. I hadn't realised that Ian had shot at such a high standard; I had never really been involved when he was doing his shooting stuff. But it was great listening to some of their stories.

Dave McCutcheon and Gary Smith, who own the haulage company Bullet Express, were another two guys who visited Ian all the way through. I'll never forget going in to see Ian on Christmas Day, and David was visiting… even though he had guests coming to his house for dinner!

Andy Rankin, Gordon Hay, and Alan Hay were always around as well. Andy would usually phone me beforehand and grab a pizza and some Cokes to take into the hospital. Sometimes there was a lot more pizza left than was actually eaten, but it was great sitting chatting to Ian and going over old stories. We had all been friends for years, so we had more than enough material to talk and laugh about.

Two other people who visited were friends from school, Sandra Miller and Alan Beattie. I thought that was particularly kind, as Ian had probably never spoken to either of them in about twenty years. They had got wind of Ian's Illness over Facebook and wanted to pay him a visit.

Obviously, the most important people were never away from his side through all his treatment: Ian's partner, Jean, the kids, and our mother. How Jean and Mum coped through everything, I will never know. And although this story is just my own recollection of events, please never underestimate Jean and my mum's involvement in all this. Jean was by Ian's side morning, noon, and night. Often, she would over at the hospital three times in the one day, taking him meals, juices, and ice cream.

Over the Christmas period, Ian's chemo sessions seemed to get tougher, it was always the same routine: he would get his chemo, then feel really lousy for a few days; as his immune system was non-existent, he would get an infection that would completely floor him for about two weeks, be put on a high dose of antibiotics to try and fight the infection; and eventually, Ian would feel better again.

That spell was probably when Ian was at his lowest. We had all hoped he would get home for Christmas and New Year, but he caught an infection after his chemo session and this time found it really hard to shake off. I wanted to get him something nice for his Christmas and decided to buy him a Links of London bracelet. I bought two identical bracelets and decided I would give him one and I would keep the other. My idea was that we would both wear them during his illness, and hopefully one day they would bring back memories of not just the bad times but the good times we had shared in hospital, and act as a reminder that we as brothers could beat this illness.

Unfortunately, on Christmas Day, Ian was really ill and could hardly talk to me. I tried to cheer him up, but it was obvious he was not in a good place. Although he tried to rally a few times, he asked me to take the bracelets away and bring them back in a few days' when he would be feeling better.

Christmas was tough. Naturally, I wanted to enjoy a happy family occasion with my own wife and kids, but Ian was never far away from my thoughts at any time. For New Year, I had planned to take my family to Oban in North West Scotland to a log cabin for a few days. I had discussed it a few weeks previously with Ian, it was decided we should keep the booking and also take my mother with us.

There was no Wi-Fi or mobile phone signal at our cabin, so I couldn't contact him after the midnight bells taking us into 2014. But the next morning I got up at 7.30am, climbed a big hill behind the cabin, and managed to get a few reception bars on my mobile. Thankfully, I was able to call Ian and wish him a Happy New Year. It was great to hear his voice, and even better to find out that he was feeling better and had started eating again. He told me he couldn't remember me being in over Christmas and knew nothing about the bracelet. I told him he would get his present as soon as I got back the next day.

6

'Be happy for this moment, because this moment is your life.'

Omar Khayyam, *poet*

January turned out to be a good month. Ian got home from hospital a few times and was over the moon with his progress. More importantly, he only had one of the big chemo sessions left to take, so all of a sudden we could start to see light at the end of a very long tunnel. I was due to go on a stag week to Las Vegas near the end of the month, which Ian would also have been on, but it was out of the question this time. However, he did manage to go back to the Go-Karting for a few meetings with Sandy, and even bought a big touring camper van for them to travel up and down the country to the various Karting events.

From what I recall, Ian had his last big chemo session, then he was allowed to go home and only attend the hospital as a day patient.

By the time he was discharged from Monklands, Ian was looking well again, and just seemed to carry on from where he'd left off before his illness.

In my opinion, he was pushing himself too hard too quickly, but there was no stopping him and he was soon visiting his office again, doing some work from home, and taking wee Sandy to the Karting and Mini Moto motor biking.

We even began planning our proposed trip to Skye, and I told him I had booked a whole bunkhouse for the weekend of the 4th of July, then emailed friends and climbing buddies to invite anyone interested to join us. Everything was looking good.

In the first week in February, I was working at a house in Battlefield, near to the Victoria Infirmary Hospital in Glasgow. Ian had told me he was going for the results of the scans which had been carried out after he left Monklands Hospital.

When my phone rang, I went outside and answered the call with my heart in my mouth. A jubilant Ian said his scans were clear, the doctors expected him to make a full recovery, and that he didn't need to go back to hospital for further tests for another 12 weeks.

On hearing his news, I admit I just broke down, and ended up hanging up on Ian, although I am sure he could tell from my reaction the way I felt. In one brief phone call, all the horrible feelings I'd had at the start just disappeared, along with the nightly visits to hospital, the Christmas and New Year at Monklands, the smuggled pizzas, carry-out McDonalds, the Sweetheart stouts, the breakout for an Indian meal, the five-and-a-half months of hell. It all just disappeared.

We had beaten this; or should I say, Ian had beaten this. He had walked into hospital with a stomach complaint, found out he might have to be ripped opened, eventually been told he was carrying Burkett's Lymphoma around with him, and now he had walked out clear. Ian was definitely my hero that day.

Anyone who is living with cancer or who has close relatives going through this, will know exactly how we felt. Life feels as though it's a dream – or nightmare; you get on with work, but everything is secondary. The only thing that keeps coming back into your mind every few minutes is cancer.

Obviously, I now know that Ian was not in the all-clear zone, and there is a nagging doubt in my head that Ian only told us what WE wanted to hear, or maybe Ian had just heard what HE wanted to hear. How could someone give him the all-clear a week after his last round of treatment? Looking back now, I am sure in my own mind that the 12-week check-up would probably be the first indication of whether the disease was gone or not. But as always, I took Ian's word for it and believed exactly what he told us, and I emailed and texted everyone I knew to let them know he was on the mend.

Ian Horne was back!!!!

7

'A new beginning stands before us, like a chapter in a book waiting to be written; we can help write that story by setting goals.'

Melody Beattie, *author*

A few weeks passed, and Ian started to get back to his old life again. He would pop in to see us every other day, he was back contacting work colleagues and, as usual, doing far too much.

We decided that climbing the Inaccessible Pinnacle on the Isle of Skye was going to be our goal, but for that we would need to get Ian back out on the hills to get hill fitness and build up his confidence again. As soon as I could, I took Ian back out walking and suggested we climb Tinto Hill the following Saturday. This was the local hill which Ian had said he would just be glad to get up again when he was undergoing treatment in hospital, never mind the Inaccessible Pinnacle.

The week before I was at one of the plumbing merchants in Glasgow and a guy in a 4x4 pulled up and asked if I knew where Glasgow Climbing Centre was, and could I direct him. His car had a CAC logo on it, and I got talking to him about climbing. CAC is a charity and it stands for Climbers against Cancer. I had never heard of the charity before, and the guy was going to an event at the climbing centre. I pointed him in the right direction and when I got home I looked the charity up online and purchased a few hoodies and t-shirts from their online shop.

The hoodies and t-shirts arrived a few days before the Tinto climb, so it was great that we managed to wear them when we climbed the hill that day. Wee Sandy was always by his dad's side, so it was only natural that we brought him along. We just took our time and had a few good rests on the way up. In fact, I was glad that Sandy had come along because it meant the pace was perfect for Ian.

On the way up, we climbed over a gate or style, and I noticed that Ian appeared to have his beer belly back. Without thinking, I began winding him up about it and said, 'I see you're not long in getting your beer belly back.' The minute I said it, we both just looked at each other and I think we were sharing the same thought: *Ian had not been drinking since he'd got home from hospital, so it couldn't be a beer belly.*

We ignored the comment and got to the top of the hill, where we got a great photograph of the three of us. Tinto is an average hill, and probably about an hour and a half can easily get you to the top. After all Ian had been through, we were delighted to get there, and enjoyed sitting for a while to have a bite to eat and a drink before heading back down.

The following week, Ian managed to take Sandy to Ben Lawers, another Munro mountain, near the town of Killin near Loch Lomond, but he only managed to get to about 800m before there was no visibility and there was a white-out on the snow-covered hill. Sandy loved it and they got some great pictures showing them kitted out from head to toe in the same gear.

We spoke about the Isle of Skye climb again and decided we would try and make a training schedule for both of us.

Ian was now back into his karting again with Sandy, which meant he only had one weekend free a month. So we decided that we would use the free weekend to climb a hill, and in-between times, Ian would just try and get out walking as much as he could.

March seemed to fly by. We got no walking or climbing done with Ian, but I had organised a climbing weekend in Spain with a load of climbing friends thinking Ian would come along – if not fit for the climbing, just so he could get some sun on his back and get some walking done. But he said he just had too much going on. Sandy was back in full swing with Karts and Mini Moto, and Ian was helping his older son, Dillon, through his motorbike test.

8

*'Trust your instinct. And if you can't tell what your instinct
is telling you, learn to peel back the noise in your life that is
keeping you from hearing it.'*

Caroline Ghosn, *American businesswoman*

I knew that April was always going to be an important month because Ian was due to go back to hospital for his twelve-week appointment, and to be honest, I had my doubts about his all-clear result. He hadn't really gained much weight, he was always sore, and found it difficult to get up and move around freely, although he could put on a good performance and kept telling me he had never felt better. Unknown to me, shortly after the Tinto Hill climb and the remark about his beer belly, Ian had started experiencing night sweats again, his stomach was gradually becoming hard and swollen again, and all the original symptoms were coming back. Without my knowledge, he had gone back to hospital for more tests and was awaiting the results.

Around lunchtime on the 10th April, my phone rang. It was Ian to let me know he had just left a meeting at the hospital, where he'd been told that the cancer was back. The test results had come back positive.

I was stunned, but realised that my gut feeling and instincts had been correct. Calmly, though, I asked what could be done. Ian said there were a few options but couldn't confirm anything until he had another meeting with all the consultants the following Monday.

Obviously, that weekend dragged by for us all. Ian's meeting was arranged for 11am on Monday 14th April; it was the Easter holiday break and the schools were off.

The consultants had asked for Ian's partner Jean to go along to the Monday meeting, so they arranged for young Sandy to go to my mum's and their daughter Sara to Jean's mum's. The kids had no idea where their parents were going, and Ian hadn't told our own mother either. 'No point in worrying her,' he said.

That day, I was working in the town of Kilbirnie in Ayrshire, and found myself clock-watching from 11am onwards. Every time my phone went, I hoped it was Ian with some good news. It wasn't until around 1 o'clock that the call finally came through.

Ian was very calm during the call. He explained that the meeting had gone as he'd expected and there was nothing more the doctors could do. Basically, he told me, he had two options.

1. To go back to hospital and undergo treatment that would prolong his life maybe four to six months, or

2. Go home, spend some quality time with Jean and his family, and be treated when necessary.

I asked Ian how long he reckoned he had before he would end up bed-bound, and was told roughly four to six weeks. In his opinion, the only option was to come home, spend some quality time with us, and never surrender to this horrible illness.

Immediately, my mind went back to the time I'd visited Ian

in the hospital when he'd pointed out a fellow patient playing cards with his son, and said the man was just being given a bag of pills to go home with. It seemed that was Ian was facing the same outcome.

9

'Create memories that last a lifetime, make an impression on the world, dream about unrealistic goals and make them reality.'

Anonymous

Ian wasted no time in making a list of things he wanted to do in what time he had left. The top three were:

1. To take Jean and the kids to London to see the sights and let the kids see Buckingham Palace.

2. Climb the Inaccessible Pinnacle on the Isle of Skye with me.

3. To catch another salmon in the River Lochy with his fishing friends up in Fort William.

Ian had spoken to me when in hospital about never having taken the kids down to London, which I honestly found bizarre because he had travelled all over and I had presumed he would have taken them down at some point. I told Ian to organise and try to get down to London as soon as he could, and to worry about the rest later.

He was due to go back into hospital for some treatment on the Wednesday and he was taking Sandy to a local Karting event on the Saturday, so the earliest he was going to get to London with Jean and the kids would be the following week.

But on the Thursday, one of his three wishes – along with

one of mine – was about to come true.

I looked at the weather forecast for the Isle of Skye and the conditions were almost perfect for climbing up there the following day, which was the Friday. I didn't think Ian was anywhere near fit enough to do the climb, as he had not done much training beforehand, but then I just thought, *Fuck it! We can only give it a good shot and see how it goes.*

The Friday was the 18th of April, Good Friday, and it was also going to be Ian's 47th birthday. I phoned him on the Thursday lunchtime and told him about the forecast, and pointed out that we would probably never get a chance to climb the Inaccessible Pinnacle again. He said he would phone me back in ten minutes.

I then phoned my cousin John Brown and told him of my plan to leave with Ian later that day, we would head up and bunk somewhere in Skye, and climb on the Friday. Immediately, John said he would come along.

When Ian returned my call, he said he would love to come along, but the only thing troubling him was that our cousin John was coming to see him that night and he didn't want to miss him. I told him not to worry, John was coming with us.

He broke down on the phone, but it was just him being happy that John was going to be with us.

*

I went straight home and got all the ropes, harnesses, and kit organised, and then picked Ian up and drove to John's house. Ian decided he wanted to drive; he wasn't drinking, so he said it would allow John and me to relax and have a few beers on the five-hour journey. He probably shouldn't have been allowed to drive with all the drugs he was taking, but who was I to say no?

Ian drove all the way up, and I remember looking at him as

he was cursing some slow driver and thinking, *This is surreal. We are heading to climb in Skye, there is a fair chance you're not going to be with us in a few weeks, and here you are cursing a Driving Miss Daisy!*

We had a great laugh on the journey, chatting and reminiscing about things we had all done, and at no point would you have looked at Ian and imagined what he was going through.

We had phoned ahead and managed to get a room at the Sligachan Bunk House. By the time we got there, it was about 11pm, so we quickly got our key, headed over to the pub for last orders, and managed to relax with a pint and enjoy a Rusty Nail (Whisky & Drambuie mix).

*

When we woke it was 18th April, Good Friday, and Ian's 47th birthday. Instead of spending his last birthday with his family, Ian was with me and our cousin John, and for that I will always be grateful to Jean and the kids. I will never forget it.

At breakfast, I could not believe the amount of pills Ian had to take before leaving that morning. I had no idea what they were all for, but he said he needed to take them to help get him through the day.

We then set off up our mountain to try and achieve what we set out to do. I deliberately set off at a slow pace, but Ian being Ian was happy to go at a faster pace. It wasn't long, though, before we had to slow down and take a few rest stops. I kept encouraging him along the way, telling him we would stop at the next big rock or where the path splits.

At one point, he just wanted a really good stop and a lie down, which was fine as we had all day. So, we just sat and admired where we were, we watched the sea and the waves crashing against the shore and spoke about how far we had come – not only up the mountain, but as brothers. I'm not ashamed to admit there were a few wee tears shed, then Ian was back on his feet again and heading for the midway point.

John liked to walk a bit ahead, because he tended to stiffen up if he stopped, so he always seemed to be that wee bit in front of us.

We got further up, and from memory I was convinced we only had to climb one more large rock and the Inaccessible Pinnacle was going to be in front of us. I got Ian behind me, and kept telling him it was just over this top. As usual, though, it wasn't. But on the positive side, we could see the top of the Pinn in the distance.

Ian's face lit up and he seemed to get so much more energy. Before we knew it, we had done what we set out to do and had reached the Inaccessible Pinnacle. All we had to do now was get our ropes out and climb the damn thing.

John had a look and decided it was not for him; not that day, anyway. He said he would just stay down and take some photos and video footage.

Both Ian and I got roped up and headed to the bottom to start the climb. I led and belayed Ian up about three pitches, then I climbed up to the last section. It is probably the easiest part of the climb, but at the same time, if you fall either side it would take a wee while before you hit the ground.

Ian had asked me to lead the climb that day. Between the two of us, I was probably the more experienced climber, but make no mistake, Ian was a pretty competent climber as well. At this point, however, I did something that I would never ever do elsewhere or with anyone else – for the last section I didn't tie myself in or secure myself to anything. I was still attached to Ian on a rope, so in theory, if Ian had slipped or fallen, he would have taken me with him and we would have been seeing the Grim Reaper together. Looking back now, it was stupid, but I trusted Ian with my life and I wanted to show him that.

When he got to the top, he asked me to come over to where he was standing, and looked up at the sky. 'Do you realise, Allan, this is the closest we are ever going to get to heaven together?' he joked.

In reply, I just showed him my untied rope and said, 'You're not half kidding, Ian. If you'd fallen, we were both on our way quicker than you thought.'

He just looked at me and shook his head, then announced, 'C'mon, let's abseil off this fucker and get down to the pub!'

Just as he was about to abseil down, he added, 'I'm absolutely shitting myself, but do you know why I love doing this with you? Because it makes me feel alive! See you at the bottom.' And away he went.

To this day, I have no idea how Ian managed to achieve this feat. Later in the year, I took a group of friends back up and we went the same route. Hardly any of them could believe how Ian had not only managed to get there but how he managed to climb the Inaccessible Pinnacle then get back down safely. Maybe just sometimes, when you believe in something you think is impossible, it actually becomes possible. At no point did I think Ian would not get up there, but the speed, determination, and the will he showed that day was a lesson I will never forget. To stand on top of the Inaccessible Pinnacle with him by my side, and for me to do all his ropes for him, is something else I will never forget. Ian was more than capable of doing all his own ropes, but that day he insisted I led the climb and that I tie his ropes for him. Maybe he was just being lazy, but I honestly think he just wanted to put his trust in me once more and allow me to show him the way, rather than the usual other way round.

Again, Ian drove on the way home, and we stopped off at three places. First, I wanted to show Ian and John the view from the Glen Garry Viewpoint carpark, if you look North at the lochs in the distance they look very much like the map of Scotland. Ian and John had never seen or noticed this before,

The next place we stopped at was the Commando Monument at Shiel Bridge. John was once in the Forces, and as a family we have always been proud that we had and still do have friends and family in the Armed Forces.

We got a great picture of the three of us at the monument. It was one of my last pictures with Ian and one of my most precious.

The third place we stopped at was Ian's old hunting ground, Camisky House in Torlundy, just outside Fort William.

Camisky House is where Ian had worked for large periods of time over the past few years as a fishing ghillie with John Veitch (who presented him with the picture of the River Lochy while he was a patient in Monklands Hospital), and it was great to have dinner with John and his family before we headed home later on the Friday night.

*

Ian had to be home and up early on the Saturday as there was a karting event on that weekend, and by coincidence it was at Larkhall, our home town. Ian had decided that the time alone dedicated to the sport meant it had to end, never mind having to bankroll this crazy sport.

That weekend was to be Sandy's final karting weekend in the sport. So, Ian took his camper van down and set it up, just like any other karting weekend, but I had invited some mates and old friends from school down to watch and we all enjoyed a good few laughs together.

Sandy did really well, and it was great to see him qualify for the final. I think most people in the crowd were cheering him on to get into the final that day.

Near the end of the day, one of the karting dads handed me a box. They'd organised a whip-round for Ian, and there must have been about a £1000 in cash in the box, which they wanted to be put towards Ian's family trip to London.

The last thing my brother wanted was a gift, as these guys were all his friends, but he accepted it graciously and I know how much their generosity meant to him.

He finished off the day at the awards ceremony, where Sandy was given a prize for best manoeuvre of the day, and Ian got some nice family photos on the podium with the kids

That week, I remember the weather was really good and on the Monday Ian phoned to ask where I was. He had just picked up a sports car from a friend at the karting – a Lamborghini Diablo – and popped over to the house to take me for a run and to give me a shot at driving this beast of a car. His friend had let him borrow it for the day.

Probably a lot of people's bucket lists would include driving a high-powered sports car, but I was just happy to be a passenger in it, so I passed on the shot to Ian's oldest son, Dillon. It was certainly a nice car to have for the day, but it was bizarre to think Ian let Dillon drive it even though he hadn't even passed his driving test.

Now, it was time for Ian to head off to London and enjoy a few days with Jean and the kids.

10

Our friends, David McCutcheon and Gary Smith, who own the haulage company Bullet Express, have a hospitality vehicle which is all kitted out to take guests to corporate events.

With true generosity, they arranged for one of their drivers to take Ian and his family to London in the hospitality vehicle. They ended up staying near Reading in Hampshire, which was great for two reasons, Joe, who was Ian's driver for the trip, got to see his sister who lives in the town, and Ian got to meet close family friend, Tania Degiorgio, and our cousin David Horne – both of whom live in Reading.

Ian, Jean, and the kids had a great few days in London, and got some great photos visiting the palace, Big Ben, Trafalgar Square, the London Eye, and all the usual tourist sights. They then carried on to Lego Land where the kids especially wanted to visit. Ian looked really well in the photographs, and Jean said he got through the week with no real problems. He looked as though he had been given a new lease of life, never mind being told he only had weeks to live.

When Ian returned home, however, he started to feel unwell again and it looked as though he had caught another infection. He was prescribed another round of antibiotics and then sent back home from hospital.

David and Gary had invited Ian along to Cameron House Hotel at Loch Lomond, as they were playing in a golf match there. Ian asked me to come along as well, and if I would drive.

I had to get suited and booted to go along, as we were due to have a champagne lunch and sail down Loch Lomond on Gary's boat after the golf, and Ian was feeling better and looking forward to it.

Initially, it was arranged I would pick Ian up at his house at 11.30am, then he gave me a call to put it back to 12.30. Then it all changed again, and he told me to meet him at Monklands Hospital at 1pm.

I arrived fifteen minutes early, so I headed to the canteen for a quick snack, and Ian text me to say he was waiting for me in the family room in Ward 16.

When I got there, I was surprised to see my mother, but I was asked to come into the room and shut the door. Ian didn't look too good, to be honest; his stomach had swollen again and he was really sweating.

As he was clearly not up to travelling to Cameron House Hotel, he admitted that the real reason he'd invited me there was to ask me to be his best man. He had asked Jean to marry him when they were in London, and she had said yes. But now, Ian had taken a turn for the worse and was going to be admitted straight back into hospital.

He then told me the news I did not want to hear. When he'd told the doctors of his plans to marry two weeks later – May 31st – they'd assured him they would do everything they could to keep him alive until the wedding, but they could not be sure he would make it. And if he did, they could not guarantee what kind of shape he would be in.

Ian told me, 'Looks like we have climbed our last mountain together, Allan, but would you do me the honour of being best man at my wedding? The doctors will keep me going, so trust me, I will be there before, during, and after the wedding.'

To be asked to be best man by anyone is always an honour; to be asked under these circumstances was a bit surreal. But it was the most wonderful thing Ian had ever asked me.

Of course, I would! I would be the best fucking man there ever was!

11

'No matter the days of anxiety that come our way, we shall emerge stronger because of the trials to be overcome.'

Bill Struth, *former manager, Glasgow Rangers FC*

Every year in May, I take my family to Crete on holiday, and that year we were due to go from 17th to 24th May -- a trip we'd booked before Ian's illness.

Torn about whether to go or not, I discussed it with my family, and with Jean and Ian. In the end, it was decided we should go ahead. I knew there were daily flights back to the UK, so if anything happened, I could be home by the next day at the latest. The break would also give me time to organise some sort of Stag Day for Ian, and the opportunity to prepare a speech for his wedding.

When we were out in Crete, I was never off the phone to Ian. But I was also in touch with all our friends, organising a Stag Day at Ibrox Stadium, home of our football team, Glasgow Rangers. Ten years previously, Ian and I played in a charity match there, and I wanted to go back there with him and his boys. I was determined to make it one of the most unforgettable days of our lives.

While the family enjoyed the time in Crete, my mind was always elsewhere. Thankfully, my wife was understanding about the time I spent on the phone, and jotting down notes for the Stag Day, the wedding, and my speech.

During the holiday, I decided I wanted to have a tattoo done, with Ian in mind. I settled on having a picture of Johnny Cash tattooed on my arm, with my brother's initials tattooed into the guitar Johnny Cash was leaning against. Ian had always liked Johnny Cash, his stories of life, and his religious beliefs. When we were up in the Isle of Skye doing the climb, he had spoken to me about Johnny Cash being 'a walking contradiction'. It was a phrase which came from a song which Kris Kristofferson wrote, partly about his friend and fellow musician, called *The Pilgrim, Chapter 33*.
The song includes the lines:

> *'He's a walking contradiction,*
> *partly truth and partly fiction,*
> *Taking every wrong direction*
> *on his lonely walk back home.'*

In many ways, the words applied to Ian. Like Johnny Cash, Ian never always did what he preached, but deep down he was a hell of a nice guy, and if you were honest and truthful to Ian, by God, he was tenfold back. Ian would never take the easy path, the path others followed, and he was very single-minded. Some people might see that as a fault, but it was one of his strengths. He was seldom wrong, and when he focused on something he needed to do or get done, then you could guarantee it got done.

I also got the words 'A Walking Contradiction' inked into the tattoo.

When the tattoo was done, I took some photos of it and sent them to Ian. Andy Rankin was with him when he received the pictures, and from what Andy said about Ian's reaction, you can't buy those moments.

I would probably never even have thought about a Johnny Cash tattoo before, but it's one of the best things I have ever done.

*

For the Stag Day, I had arranged for us all to meet at Rangers' stadium, where we would get a small tour of the building, followed by a meal in the Argyle Suite overlooking the pitch.

As I had just come back from Crete, I had not seen Ian in a week and got quite a shock when he appeared in the trophy room a little late. He looked really ill. In fact, some of the guys at the Stag Day who hadn't seen him in a while did not recognise him; they were just stunned at how much weight he had lost.

For most of the stadium tour, Ian just sat out on a seat. He did what he could, but I could tell he was really feeling lousy, and I was starting to wish I had never organised anything.

We managed to get a photo of him with all the boys on the famous marble steps of the main stand, where Ian stood and started a chorus of the Rangers' song, 'I'm Rangers till I Die'. In the circumstances, it probably wasn't in the best taste, but it was Ian who started it off and we all sang along. He managed to rally a bit for the meal, and managed an off-the-cuff speech thanking everyone for coming and looking forward to seeing them at his wedding the following Friday. Jean then came and collected him, and took him back to the house.

*

The next few days, Ian was back in hospital and was not great on the Monday or Tuesday, but when I went in to visit him on the Wednesday he was feeling a lot better, laughing and joking, and saying he'd had some good news from test results.

David McCutcheon had also come up to visit, and in conversation he explained that his company Bullet Express was organising a charity cycle ride. The staff, apparently, had a static fitness bike in the office and were going to take it in turns to cycle on the bike and see how long it took them to cover the equivalent of a journey from Land's End to John o' Groats – 874 miles.

Jokingly, I suggested I would go to Land's End on my bike for real and race against his office staff, and see how much money we could raise for charity.

Ian thought it was a brilliant idea and asked if the money could to go to the Macmillan Nurses – a charity organisation set up to help cancer patients and their families.

Later that night, David phoned and asked if I really would be up for the challenge, and I immediately said yes. Ian needed to have something to focus on, and I desperately wanted him to be there at the end when I finished at John o' Groats. I was determined to try everything possible to keep my brother alive, even if it was just for a few more weeks.

We agreed on a date of 19th June for the start of the bike ride, and I estimated it would take me nine days to complete – roughly one hundred miles a day. So, David and Gary got on with organising the trip, and I concentrated on Ian's wedding which was in just two days' time.

It was obviously going to be a small family wedding, and we had decided to wear Highland dress for the occasion. Trying to source about 15 kilts in the same tartan in such a short space of time was always going to be a tall order, but strangely enough, after I'd contacted almost every Highland dress business in Glasgow with no success, Jean phoned and said she had sourced them in a shop not more than 500 yards from Monklands Hospital.

Sometimes, things just happen.

We had arranged that Ian and Jean would be married in Hamilton Town Hall, followed by dinner at the Avonbridge Hotel in Hamilton. Ian then wanted an open-door reception for everyone at the Applebank Inn in Larkhall.

The Applebank Inn has a special place in our family. It was the first pub Ian and I ever drank in; it was Ian's local pub for years; all the christening parties for our children were celebrated there; and I held my engagement party there. Ian wanted everyone to come along, and told me he wanted to offer a free bar, including for any of the locals who had just popped down for a night out.

On the Thursday, the day before the wedding, Ian took ill again. This time, he was so poorly that the doctors said he wouldn't be able to attend his own wedding. In their view, if Ian wanted to get married, it was going to have to be in hospital.

I was in the room with Ian and Jean when he had just been told, and they were naturally both devastated. Determined that they would have their special day, I told them, 'Ok, guys, I know it's not ideal, but let's get our heads round this and change a few things.'

Our new plan involved:

- Cancelling Hamilton Town Hall, and seeing if we could get the Registrar to come to Monklands Hospital;

- Cancelling the Avonbridge Hotel, and I would see if the Applebank could take us all for our meals there;

- And enquiring if there was somewhere within Monklands Hospital where Ian and Jean could actually get married.

Once again, everything fell into place.

In Monklands Hospital, there is a drop-in centre for cancer patients and family called the Maggie's Centre. Although it had not officially opened yet, they assured us they would have no problem in Ian and Jean getting married there.

Hamilton Town Hall – cancelled!

I then spoke to Audrey Lockhart, the owner of the Applebank Inn, and she had no problem whatsoever about taking us all for the wedding dinner.

Avonbridge Hotel cancelled!

And the Registrar confirmed that she was able to come to the hospital and marry Ian and Jean there.

Wedding venue sorted.

Everyone was given the new information about the changes of venue, and it was all systems go for the big day.

11

'Love recognizes no barriers. It jumps hurdles, leaps fences,
penetrates walls, to arrive at its destination full of hope.'

Maya Angelou, *author*

Friday, May 31, 2014 was Ian and Jean's wedding day. I had told Ian I was going to come up to the hospital early and spend time with him so we could help each other get dressed for the 1pm ceremony.

I got up early that morning and headed up to Ian and Jean's house to see the bride and to collect a few things. All the girls were there getting ready with the hair and makeup, and I shared a wee glass of champagne with them before heading over to the hospital.

Ian was not too good and I had hoped to see him in better shape, even if it meant the doctors drugging him up. But to be honest, nothing was going to stop him getting out his bed and walking down the aisle to get married.

I had taken up a couple of bottles of champagne, thinking we could get a wee glass of bubbly with the nurses, without even thinking that of course the nurses would never be able to have a drink on duty.

When I arrived, some of the nurses asked me to come with them for a second. They had prepared a whole section of the ward for us to come back to after Ian and Jean had tied the knot. They had moved all the beds out of one of the rooms, had completely done the whole place up with balloons, and set out some tables and chairs. And unbeknown to us, the nurses and doctors had clubbed together and provided a buffet, complete with bottles of cava and champagne.

It was a lovely gesture and totally unexpected! I can't thank the nurses enough for what they did, not only that day but from the minute Ian had arrived at Monklands Hospital in the October. We knew, and everyone there knew, it was not going to be the outcome we had hoped for, but how these guys do that job every day is unbelievable. To see people given hope and being part of that must be very satisfying, but at the same time being part of the other side must be completely heart-breaking.

As Ian had been there so long, he knew all the staff, where they were from, about their families – and they knew all about him.

As we got ready that day, one by one they came in and wished us luck, and nearly all left with tears in their eyes.

Ian wanted me to help him get washed and shaved, but it was proving quite slow and I always had one eye on the clock. Eventually, I had to admit defeat and ask a couple of nurses to come in and help. I still had to get ready, too, so I went round to the wedding room and got changed there, where a few nurses helped me as well. It's harder to dress in a kilt than you think!

When I went back to get Ian, he was all ready and smiling. First, I took him round to the room which the nurses had prepared for us, and he could not believe it. Another wee tear came to his eye, and we got some photos together. The hospital even sent up their own photographer, so we got a load of pictures with the nurses, and then we were off to the Maggie's Centre to see my brother get married.

The nurses gave me a wheelchair to take Ian over, and he had to have a nurse come with us. We took the car to go from the main building to the Maggie's Centre and I drove. Halfway there, the nurse pointed out that she was sure she had seen me drink about four glasses of champagne, so I probably shouldn't have been driving. Ian just reminded me what he had said a few months ago about using his name and address if I got stopped.

When we got over to the centre, we were completely gobsmacked. It was a great place to get married. The entrance to the building is beautiful, and the staff had prepared the reception area with more bubbly, while the main wedding area was as nice as any venue.

We got loads of pictures outside, and Ian wanted to get out of the wheelchair. I helped him up and got him inside, where he managed to walk down the aisle and get married.

Everyone that should have been there was there. The men all had our kilts on, and the women all looked great in their wedding outfits.

Everything went to plan. Ian and Jean said their vows, then Ian gave a wee toast and invited everyone back up to Ward 16. When we got back up to the ward, everyone had a wee drink and then I was asked to give my best man speech.

I had prepared it while I was away in Crete and, unlike the usual best man speeches, there was no piss-taking. I just wanted to let Ian know how grateful I was to him for the life he had given me.

He had let me run with him since I was a kid, we had done almost everything together, and I just wanted to express how much we had achieved and shared as brothers.

I am sure the feelings were passed on to him, feelings he didn't need to be told as he knew exactly how I felt.

Ian again made a toast and another great speech as a reply. I've always believed it was the mark of the guy, how he could just deliver speeches and replies off-the-cuff and get the feeling through to everyone. Ian was an absolute genius at that sort of thing.

We had booked the Applebank Inn from 4pm, so it was time for everyone to head over there.

Ian had to stay in hospital and get more treatment, but we were assured he would be allowed to travel over to Larkhall later for a couple of hours for the reception. Again, David and Gary organised the hospitality people carrier to collect him later, along with one of the nurses.

That night at the Applebank Inn will be another night I will never forget as long as I live. I have never seen the pub as busy, and the weather was stunning.

Ian came over as promised at 8pm, and it was great seeing everyone there. Alaistair, our local minister, had been invited down and he gave another wedding blessing on the steps of the Applebank. I don't think in all the history of the Applebank Inn, anyone will have seen anything like it.

It was an amazing night and, after seeing Ian the past few days, it was even more incredible that everything went as planned.

Ian stayed until about 11pm then he had to go back to hospital. It was very emotional when he left the reception, as I am sure most of the guests in the back of their minds would be thinking it might be the last they would see of my brother.

*

But over that weekend, Ian really perked up and was in great form up at the hospital. He was laughing and joking and was buzzing about the wedding, so we started discussing the charity bike ride I was going to do. He wanted me to donate any money raised to Macmillan and the Maggie's Centre, for all that they had done for him.

With everything that had been going on in the run-up to the wedding, I had not really been on my bike much, so I managed to get a run on the Sunday morning after the wedding. It was only 30 miles, but I had another two weeks to prepare, and I wanted to build my training up to a couple of 70 or 80-mile runs.

I went on a cycle on the Tuesday and deliberately headed over to the hospital for a visit and back, which took me over the 50-mile mark.

Ian was also buzzing about the bike ride and he wanted to be at John o' Groats when I finished. He joked with me that the doctors had thought he would be dead by now, but he had already proved them wrong. He also revealed that he was to be given some different drugs, and someone had told him they knew people who had taken them for months after being told they had only days to live. Ian wanted to prove everyone wrong and be there for the end of my cycle. For my part, I told him I wanted him to be around for a lot longer than the end of my cycle ride, and hoped we would be exchanging Christmas gifts for a few more years to come yet.

I had decided to do a full day cycle on the Saturday as training, and my aim was to get 100 miles under my belt. I knew that if I could do 100 miles, I would be okay for anything the actual bike ride would throw at me. I had done a few five-day cycle runs in the past, and remembered thinking after day three all the muscle and mental pain goes away. You still cramp up when you finish, but after day three you can basically ride all day, as long as you rehydrate and keep eating. The most I had ridden in the last couple of years, though, was an 85-mile run at an Etape Caledonia challenge near Pitlochry.

In the end, I think I managed about 85 miles that Saturday, during which time I got a phone call from Jean with the brilliant news that Ian was getting out of hospital. She asked if I could go and collect him, but unfortunately I was cycling through Ayrshire at the time. What happened next for our poor Ian must have been like a comedy sketch.

Jean went up to collect him, along with their daughter, Sara. When they arrived, the nurses were just finishing off his final preparations to go home, and they had to take one of the lines out his hand or arm. As soon as young Sara saw the blood, she fainted, whacked her head off the bottom of the bed, and knocked herself out.

Ian was still allowed out, but the first thing he had to do was go and sit in Accident and Emergency for four hours waiting on Sara coming round and be given the all-clear for HER to be allowed to go home!

I know you shouldn't laugh, but when I heard the story I was in stitches. Poor Ian had been waiting to get out the hospital for nearly two weeks, then ended up having to sit in the Accident and Emergency department!

I finished my bike ride and gave Ian a call later that Saturday night to hear about all the drama. I told him I would come up the next day and spend some time with him, and he was looking forward to it.

About lunchtime that Sunday, when I called and told him I was coming over, he asked if I could leave it a while as he was not feeling too great and just wanted a wee lie down. 'Ok, no problem,' I said. 'I'll give you a phone later.'

When I called later, he told me just to leave it as he had been sick again and was just wanting to sleep. 'Ok,' I told him. 'I'll be up in the morning, like it or not.'

About 11pm that same night, Jean called me. She was really distressed and asked if I could come over right away. Ian had been sick all day and could hardly move, and I think Jean was at her wits' end. She had been cleaning up his mess most of the day, and that's why Ian hadn't wanted me to come and visit. At that point, we hadn't yet discussed whether Ian had to get home palliative care. Although we knew it would be on the cards at some stage, until that point we were all coping as best as we could.

I drove straight up and could see Jean was in a bit of a state. She asked if I could take Ian back to the hospital, because she just wanted him settled. He was a bit all over the place, and wasn't keen to go.

We more or less begged Ian to let me take him back over to Hospital. I tried to explain that by going back to hospital, he would get sorted and Jean would get a wee break from all the cleaning up. 'Allan, I feel if I come out this bed and leave the house, I won't be back,' he said.

'Bullshit!' I told him. 'I just need you back over to the hospital. Let them get you back on some antibiotics, we will get you strong again, and we can get you back to the house.'

Eventually, we got him up and dressed. Looking at how weak he was completely floored me, but I didn't want to let Ian or Jean know how I was feeling. It took the two of us to get him out the bed and down the stairs. When Ian was fit and healthy, it would be quite easy to give him a hand to get out of bed or down some stairs, but when you could see how little there was of him, how fragile he was, I was just scared we hurt him. He was just skin and bone. I'd helped him get showered for his wedding and had seen how little there was of him then. Now, some nine days later, he was a lot worse.

As we made our way gradually downstairs, I remember noticing how he kept looking around the house, staring at everything, and when we got to the bottom, he just wanted to sit on the last step and take it all in.

Jean and I were pleading with him, 'Come on, Ian, let's get in the car. Please, let's just get in the car.'

I wish now we had spent just a wee while longer there; after all, what difference would a few minutes more have made? But I had insisted, even rushed him to get up and in the car. What I did not know then was that I was about to drive my brother to hospital for the very last time. Everyone says I did the right thing taking him back there, but Ian knew what was happening. He knew this was the last look at the house Ian and Jean had built together; Ian knew he was not coming back. And no matter what anyone says, I rushed Ian off that step and into the car.

That haunts me at times. Instead of letting him do what he wanted, I forced his hand and made him get up and get in the car.

I got Ian into the passenger seat with a woollen hat on and a blanket to keep him warm, and a basin in case he was sick again.

We hadn't long set off, when he suddenly became quite calm, and started asking me about the Formula One result, and I told him there had been a bad crash involving two of the drivers. He asked if the German driver, Sebastian Vettel had got a podium, and I told him he got a third. Ian replied that it was going to be a good season. Then he asked me to stop the car.

When I did, he told me, 'Allan, this is not fair on anyone, especially Jean. When we get over to the hospital, I'm going to ask to get sent back over to the house and get palliative care set up. This just can't go on, mate, the time's up.'

I said, 'Don't be fucking stupid. We will get you to hospital and get you fixed up with the antibiotics. You will be ok.'

I started driving again and then stopped the car again. This time I just broke down for a few minutes, and I apologised to Ian. I told him I was so sorry there was nothing more I could do to help him. 'I am as helpless as I have ever been in my life for you,' I told him. 'At this point in my life, Ian, I am completely helpless. My hands are tied and I can do fuck-all, mate.'

He told me to calm down. 'Of course there is something you can do,' he told me. 'You can look after wee Sandy. He's going to be a handful, but he's going to need you to look after him. Sara will be fine,' he went on, 'Jean and her mum and sisters will look after her no problem, but I'll need you to help and look after Sandy. Take him to the football and get him into your hills. He will love rock climbing with you.'

'That's a given,' I assured him. 'Of course I'll look after him.'

We then drove to Monklands Hospital and got him back up to Ward 16.

Jean had telephoned ahead, so the nurses were all expecting us. By this time, it must have been about midnight. We got him back into his room and into bed, then all the lines were inserted and he started getting his antibiotics. I am guessing he was administered morphine or diazepam as well, because he was soon starting to chill a bit, and I sat until slowly he started to drift off and eventually went to sleep.

I phoned Jean to let her know he was settled and sleeping, then asked the nurses if he would be ok until the doctors came to see him in the morning. I also explained that he wanted to talk about palliative care, and they assured me that could all be discussed the next day.

Before I left the hospital, I popped in to tell Ian I was going home to bed and would pop back the next day after work. He was fast asleep, but I told him anyway, then headed home.

As soon as I finished work the next day, I headed over to the hospital. My mate Andy Rankin was already there, and Ian was awake and talking, but I had the feeling he didn't really want any visitors. I tried to raise his spirits by talking about the bike ride, the sponsorship page Macmillan had set up for us, and how it would be great coming into the hospital on my way up from Land's End.

The bike ride was less than two weeks away and I had arranged to go down on Thursday, June 19th – in just 10 days' time, I was going to be cycling the length of Britain.

I told Ian I had just received a £250 donation from someone called Paul, who had said that if I needed accommodation in Cheshire or Cumbria, he would sort something out. I couldn't think who this Paul was, and suggested it might be one of Bullet Express's connections.

Straight away, Ian suggested it was more likely to be my climbing mate from Manchester, Paul Craven. How did I not realise that? I still feel embarrassed that one of my close friends, Paul Craven, who lives in Cheshire and also has a house in Cumbria, had donated so much and I'd never twigged who it was. Sorry, Paul.

Ian started to feel sick again, and shortly after, Jean arrived with young Sandy. I got the feeling that Ian would prefer to be alone with them, so I asked him if he wanted me and Andy to go, and he just nodded to tell me yes.

On the way out, I stopped one of the young nurses and asked how Ian was. I admitted that I knew what his long-term outcome was going to be, but wanted to know if we were now in a life or death scenario. She explained that he was on the strongest antibiotics they could give him, and as she thought he had just picked up a wee infection, she assured me that in a day or two the drugs would help, he would feel better, and hopefully would be back home in the next week or two.

That was good, and all I wanted to hear. If she thought he would be home in the next week or two, then it meant he would be able to get involved with the bike ride. The whole reason I had set the ride up was to give him something to focus on, and it looked like that was going to work.

When I got outside, I started going over all the scenarios about the ride and bombarding Andy with lots of what if questions. But he told me just to take each day at a time, see Ian as much as I could, fit in as much training as possible, and what would be would be.

12

*'I love the man that can smile in trouble, that can gather
strength from distress, and grow brave by reflection. …
he whose heart is firm and whose conscience approves his
conduct, will pursue his principles unto death.'*

Thomas Paine, *philosopher*

Jean called me about 11pm that night to let me know that
Ian had settled down once we had left and was now asleep,
so she was heading home for the night. I was really relieved.
I could sleep easier knowing Ian was settled.

But shortly after 1am, I got a call from Ward 16. The minute
the phone started ringing and I woke, I just knew what the
call was going to be,

The nurse on the line just asked if I was Allan and if I would
be ok to come over to Ward 16, because Jean needed someone
to comfort her. I just said I'd be there within twenty minutes.

I never even asked how Ian was and the nurse never told
me. She didn't need to. I knew what the call was; I knew why
Jean needed comfort. The fight was over, and my brother Ian
was dead. He passed away shortly after midnight on the 10th
June – 47 years old; a father of three; he had just become a
grandfather; he had been married for only 10 days.

To be honest, I can't remember driving to the hospital, and
I have no idea where I even parked my car. I only remember

going to the desk, speaking to Jean and the nurses, and being given the confirmation of my brother's death.

I gave Jean a hug and asked if she was ok. She was tearful, but said she was alright.

I asked to go in and see Ian alone. When I went into the room – a place I had been in a hundred times before – he was just lying there, peaceful, no pain etched on his face, very frail and grey. To be honest, he didn't look like my brother but he looked peaceful. And as much as I wanted Ian fit and healthy, something inside made me happy that it was all over. There was never going to be any happy outcome; it had always been just a matter of where and when.

I gave him a kiss and went back out to the desk to see what we needed to do, but the nurses said the best thing was to go home, try and get some rest, and we could sort everything out later.

I took Jean back to her house where her mother was waiting on her, and sat with them for a while before heading to my own mother's house to let her know about Ian.

I think that was probably the hardest thing I have had to do in my life. Most people would agree that the last thing anyone wants is to see their kids die before them, yet here I was having to tell my mum that her oldest son was dead.

I sat with her for a while and there were hugs and tears, but I looked at my mum and I saw just how strong a woman she is. She got herself together and told me I should go home and be with my own wife and kids. I suggested she come home with me, but she said, 'No, just get round and make sure Mhairi and the kids are ok.'

As anyone could imagine, I never really slept, and in the morning I began contacting friends and relatives to let them know.

One of the worst things I had to do that day was to go back to the hospital and collect Ian's belongings. It was horrible. Instead of going in as usual and cracking a joke or cheerily greeting the staff, I had to collect a suitcase, some paperwork, and say goodbye to everyone.

I thanked all the staff and headed out of the ward with the suitcase, feeling as though everyone was staring at me as if we had failed. It was like seeing your kid tripping or falling in a school race; you try to keep your head up, but you feel like everyone is looking saying that your kid has failed. Even heading out to the car, it was as though strangers were looking at me and then glancing at the suitcase. I know it wasn't really happening, but the paranoia made me think they were.

Between then and the day of the funeral, my phone never stopped with calls, text messages, or emails about Ian.

I think by the end of the week I had received about 400 personal messages from friends and people I did not even know. I've kept a load of them, and I go back and read them from time to time.

One thing that annoys me now about myself was that I took it personally when some people I thought would have phoned me to offer their support did not.

I turned on a few family members after the funeral, and with hindsight I wish I had never said anything. I should have kept quiet and let it go, it was silly and only now, looking back, I can see people react differently in these circumstances, but at that time I thought the least they could do was to make contact with me, offer their condolences and give me their support.

A message was put up on one of the message boards on a Rangers website, and again I could not believe the number of stories posted about Ian's life, concerning trips in Europe watching the Rangers. I was with him on most of the occasions, so it was great reliving the trips, but the stories I liked most were the ones I had known nothing about. I could read them all day.

Ian undoubtedly lived life to the full. Personally, I don't like the phrase 'he lived the life of many guys'. I hate it. So what? He should have had plenty of time to live the life of many more,

Most of the things Ian did, we did together, and the thing that scares me most of all now is being alone. We just always did things together, often without any real planning. He would just phone and say, 'Fancy going to Manchester tonight to watch Manchester United?' And we did. Or I would phone him and say, 'Weather looks good for snowboarding. Fancy going tomorrow?' And we would. It's just what we did.

That kills me the most; I've lost my sidekick for ever, Snowboarding, climbing, mountain biking, football, business, friends, nights out, travelling… but most of all, I've lost and miss my brother.

*

The funeral was arranged for the following Monday at 11am, and Ian himself had arranged a few things. He had asked our cousin John, who went to the Isle of Skye with us and was a former commando, to get a military Union Jack flag to be draped over his coffin. I think he asked John when we were heading home from Skye and stopped at the commando monument.

I knew what hymns Ian wanted, and who he wanted to carry him into and out of church.

I got Sandy to lead the way into church carrying the folded Union Jack flag to the hymn, *Courage, Brother, Do Not Stumble,* and he then handed it to me to drape over Ian's coffin with the help of our cousin John.

The whole church downstairs was full, and only a few pews upstairs were available. All in all, I was told over 400 people attended the service.

I delivered a eulogy for Ian. It was easy to stand up there and talk about my brother; I could have stood and said so much more, but I think and hope I expressed to everyone there exactly how much I loved and cared for my brother.

We left to the hymn, *Lead Kindly Light*, and carried my brother shoulder-high to his final resting place in the local graveyard, where he is buried beside our father.

These two men were, and always will be, my heroes and it's fitting they are back together. There is a quote from Sir Isaac Newton, which is also engraved on some two-pound coins: 'Standing on the shoulders of giants.' The full quote is: 'If I have seen further than others, it is by standing upon the shoulders of giants.' Both Ian and my dad were certainly not big men or giants, but make no mistake, they were 'my' giants. And with the help of Ian lifting me up onto both his and my dad's shoulders, they have allowed me to see further than even they were able to. I'll get to meet them soon enough, but just now I am determined to carry on and hopefully live the life Ian never got the chance to.

*

So that was that. Ian had the funeral he wanted and had enjoyed a life many people would crave for; I had committed myself to a bike ride that I had only really been doing to try and keep his spirits up.

I was asked by a few people at the funeral if I was still going ahead with it, and if so, where people could donate to it. I was even handed cash donations that day. The ride itself was due to start in three days' time – on the Thursday – so I arranged to go and see Gary Smith and David McCutcheon the next day.

I discussed it with Jean, my wife, and all the kids, and we all agreed I should still do the ride in memory of Ian, and along with the Bullet Express employees, would try and raise as much for charity as possible.

So, with only about four or five training runs completed and all the stuff going on around me, I walked into the Bullet Express offices next day and told the guys that the ride was on. I had a flight booked to Newquay on Thursday afternoon, and a van support going down on the Wednesday night with my bike and gear.

I was about to try and ride my bike from Land's End to John o' Groats for charity in memory of Ian. I had no idea whether I would be able to do the miles we had talked about each day, and wasn't even sure why I now really wanted to do this. My whole reason initially had been to give my brother hope and to focus on seeing me complete it, but he was no longer here.

Yet I just kept thinking it was Ian and David that had asked me to do this to give something back to the nurses, and felt I had made a commitment not only to Ian, but to Maggie's, Macmillan, to Bullet Express, to the driver who was coming down with me, and to all the people who had already donated before I had even turned a wheel.

One thing I was sure about was that I really wanted to get away on my bike and be by myself, to have long days to think about the past year, about my life, and about family. The added bonus was that I was about to achieve one of my own dreams and cycle from Land's End in Cornwall to

John o' Groats in the North of Scotland, while at the same time raising as much money as I could for the Maggie's and Macmillan Nurses Charities.

So here I was, about to head down to Cornwall with virtually no training, hardly any planning, and absolutely no idea whether I could do this.

That was just Ian and me all over... **Let's go!**

Part Two

13

'Focus on the journey, not the destination, Joy is found not in the Finishing, but in the journey itself.'

Greg Anderson, *author*

The morning after Ian's funeral, I visited David and Gary at the Bullet Express offices and confirmed that I would be going ahead with the Land's End to John o' Groats cycle challenge in two days' time.

I had booked a flight to Newquay via Manchester for the Thursday lunchtime, and Bullet Express had arranged for a driver to collect all my gear and drive down the night before, then meet me at the airport in Newquay.

Joe Finnegan, who had volunteered to drive Ian, Jean, and the kids when they went down to visit London a few weeks before, offered to be the driver to help me along the way with this cycle challenge. On the Wednesday night, he collected all my gear and put it in the van, along with two bikes in case anything happened to one and I needed a replacement to fall back on.

The whole concept of this charity challenge was that I was going to go to Land's End and start cycling on the Friday; the Bullet Express staff had a static bike set up in the offices, but would not start cycling until the Monday. Their goal was to try and cycle enough miles each day on the static bike to 'catch me up'.

I had estimated that with three days' head-start I should be roughly 300 miles ahead before they even turned a pedal. But I hadn't been able to train as much as I'd hoped in the last few weeks, with everything that had happened. So, I had to go with the thought that I would pick up the fitness as I would go along. I had completed a few 100- mile rides in a day before, but never for NINE consecutive days. At that stage, I honestly had no idea whether I could manage it or not, but I was determined to give it one helluva go.

Thursday, 19th June:

On the Thursday morning, I got up and basically just got ready to travel. We'd had a really bad flood to the house a few weeks before and there was so much repair work going on that the place just looked like a building site. As everything would have to be put on hold until I got back, I had to apologise to my wife and kids for leaving them in such a mess and I felt really guilty. But I promised I would fix it all up when I got back, and have the place looking great again.

*

My flight from Glasgow to Manchester was on schedule, but I had got my timings wrong and had to wait an hour longer than I'd thought for my connecting flight to Newquay. To pass the time, I went for a bite to eat in one of the bars and got caught up with a bunch of lads heading to Benidorm on a stag do.

I sat talking to them and enjoyed a couple of pints of cider, which was probably not the ideal athlete's choice before a long cycle, but it was a warm day and I would soon be burning it off.

My connecting flight arrived in Newquay at 5pm, and Joe was waiting for me outside the airport with the van and all the gear. I had decided that because the first day from Land's

End to Exeter was approximately 125 miles and I had not had much cycling practice recently, it would be best to head off straight away and see how far I could get before it got dark. So, I asked Joe to head there straight away.

However, I hadn't really checked how far Land's End was from Newquay Airport, so it took a bit longer than I'd thought, and we didn't get there until 7pm.

I went straight to the famous Land's End sign and got some pictures there with my bike and my cycling gear on, then arranged with Joe that I would try and do about 30 miles. We agreed I would give him a call to come and get me wherever I stopped.

So, at 7.45pm I finally set off to travel the whole length of the UK! It was probably not everyone's choice of starting time, but I thought there was method in my madness.

As I set off from the Land's End visitor centre, it was a gorgeous night; a little windy, but I loved the night air and being on the bike. I immediately passed the first and last Inn in England, and headed up the hill to see how far I could get.

Travelling down to Land's End in the van with Joe, I had been carefully watching the route, knowing I would have to travel back a similar way. So I already knew I was going to have to cycle up and down rather a lot of hills.

I decided I was heading for Redruth, as that was approximately 30 miles in the direction I would be going, then got my head down and started following the road up the A30.

It started off as a nice country road, and I passed through a few villages, stopping briefly at a sign I noticed on the wall of a small village hall. It said: 'Christ Jesus came into the world to save sinners.' I took a picture of it then sat and reflected for a few moments that if Jesus could save sinners, then why not save the good ones as well?

On top of the Inaccessible Pinnacle.

Ian and I, Tower Ridge, Ben Nevis

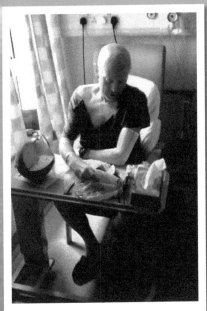

Ian ten days after being admitted
to Wishaw General.

Having a beer together in
Monklands Hospital.

Climbing Tinto Hill after getting all clear.

At the top of Tinto Hill with Sandy

Ian and Sandy on Ben Lawers

Climbing towards the Inaccessible Pinnacle.

On Cuillin Ridge.

Abseiling off the Pinnacle.

The Commando Monument at Shiel Bridge

Home dressing-room of Rangers FC

Rangers 'til I die

Ian and Jean's wedding.

Ian with the boys, Dillon and Sandy.

The Best Man and me.

Land's End

Coming home to Scotland

John O' Groats - The end
of the journey

Sandy racing in the Cool Fab Championship

Sandy Horne, Tyco BMW.

Sandy, double British Champion.

Ian climbing the Ledge Route on Ben Nevis

No one dies if they are remembered.

Immediately after I took the photo, my phone battery died. That was a real problem! All my contacts were on my phone, so how could I get in touch with Joe to collect me from Redruth when I didn't have a working phone or any contact numbers.

There was no point in worrying about it then. I decided I'd carry on and when I reached Redruth I'd find a pub and ask if they had a phone charger I could borrow.

A whole section of the A30 was closed because of roadworks heading toward Redruth, but this actually worked in my favour as I just ignored the signs and went onto the dual carriageway. It was brilliant to have the whole road to myself, though a little eerie with no traffic and not a worker in sight. It was a stunning night, and as I cycled, I watched a buzzard swooping down on something for dinner and ripping it to pieces.

The sun was going down and I arrived into Redruth just as it was getting dark. I had no idea where I was heading but came across an ambulance station next to an off-sales. I knocked at the door of the ambulance station and explained to one of the paramedics about my phone battery dying and asked if they had a charger. They did have a charger, but the guy said I wasn't allowed to go inside the station, and if the bell sounded they would have to leave immediately as that meant an emergency call and they would need to give me my phone back. I asked how many times the bell had gone that day and he said none, so I decided I would take my chance and pop into the off-sales for some crisps and a drink while my phone was charging.

As I was heading into the off-sales, the bell went off! I couldn't believe it. As I looked back, I saw the paramedic sit my phone on my bike seat then dash off. With my phone still dead, I asked the girl behind the counter of the off-sales for help, but she had no charger – not even one for sale.

The England football team were playing Uruguay in the World Cup that night, and I already knew they had been beaten as I had asked a couple of smokers as I was passing a pub earlier. The game had finished 2-0 to Uruguay, with Luis Suarez scoring both goals. So, when I headed into the town centre, the place was like a morgue. I tried two different pubs but still no charger. Trying to think of all different ways to contact Joe, I'd briefly considered a taxi… until a driver told me it would cost £120 to Newquay.

I was starving by this point and decided to go for a kebab and think out my next move. To my delight, the girl behind the counter in the kebab shop had a docking station, and she said I could plug my iPhone on there to charge.

Finally, a charger. But as I ate my kebab and waited on the phone charging, the delivery guy came in and noticed that the docking station wasn't plugged in! I was starting to think that I was not meant to get a hold of Joe at all.

Finally, after the paramedic, the off-licence, the two pubs, the attempted taxi, a kebab, and a switched-off docking station, I managed to get some power in my iPhone.

But guess what? There was no signal! I swear to God, you could not have scripted it. The girl said the top of the road was the place for a better signal, so I waited 10 minutes to charge the phone then headed up there. Eventually, I managed to call Joe, gave him the kebab shop address and postcode, and he said he would be along in half an hour. And 30 minutes later, he duly arrived and took me to my hotel in Newquay and a much-needed sleep.

What a start to an incredible journey.

13

'A disagreement or incident involving someone who is not important to you like a rude waiter, waitress or cashier is something that should roll off your shoulders. Save the effort for resolving conflicts with the people you cherish.'

Joel Osteen, *American pastor and author*

Friday, 20th June:

I had a great sleep in the Travelodge in Newquay and got up about 6.30am. The plan was to get showered, dressed and head for some breakfast at a nearby café, then Joe would drop me back off at Redruth where I would start my cycle for the next destination… Exeter.

So that morning, we headed across the road to a café near the train station for breakfast. A sign on the door said it opened at 8am, but it was only 7.50am, so we parked up and headed across. The cafe door was open, and a girl was preparing food behind the counter.

'Morning,' I said, 'any chance of two of your finest full English breakfasts, please?'

She replied, 'We open at 8am. Can you wait outside? Shut the door and come back when we are open, please.'

Lovely, I thought. *I really pity the guy who woke up next to her this morning.*

However, we headed outside, and I sat on one of the picnic tables set out for customers. When I checked my watch, it was 7.56am.

About a minute or so later, she came out and I thought she was going to take our order. But she just looked at me and said, 'Do you mind not sitting on top of the bench? People have to eat off them.'

That was it for me. I just lost it and told her to go fuck herself, I'd rather starve than eat in her café, then Joe and I walked up the street looking for somewhere else. If anyone has been to Newquay, there are not actually too many places that serve breakfasts at 8am – well, not that we could find, anyway. By this point I was starving, and started thinking that perhaps I should not have been too hard on the young lady. We decided to cut our losses and head back to Redruth, where we would hopefully find a lovely little café.

Later that night, I googled the Newquay café reviews on Trip Advisor to see what came up. And I couldn't help but have a wee laugh at some of the reviews:

1. ****, Smile a bit

2. Very poor

3. Attitude leaves a lot to be desired

4. Great amount of food but, jeez ,cheer up

5. Vile

6. Horrid service

7. Horrible woman horrible food

8. Worst customer care ever.

Obviously, there were more comments and some people had written nice things, but it seemed crazy to me how people could act like that when serving the public.

Anyway, in Redruth we found somewhere there fairly easily, the service was perfect, and we had a table set outside for a great wee fry-up before I went on my way and Joe headed away in the van for Exeter.

At the start of the cycle, I had received a message from David at Bullet Express to say that he'd been along to our local radio station (Radio Clyde) on the Thursday and been interviewed for a local news item regarding my bike ride. So, the ride would be mentioned in all the news bulletins that (Friday) morning. And right enough, I had only just set off when I started getting text messages through saying I had been mentioned on the radio along with details about the Macmillan Charity webpage. Obviously, being in Cornwall, I wouldn't be able to hear Radio Clyde, but someone kindly sent me the recording of it via my iPhone.

I felt chuffed that it would help the charity and it gave me a boost as I headed on the long journey to Exeter.

The first part of the cycle was great, and I cruised along the roads over to Truro and onto the A390. I was heading to St Austell when I passed a house that was completely decked out in England flags, obviously because the World Cup was on at that time. England had been beaten the night before and, being Scottish, I could not help but stop and take a selfie outside the guy's house with all the flags in the background.

Further along my journey, I saw a sign for the Eden Project. Regarded as the Eighth Wonder of the World by some, the Eden Project is a 'dramatic global garden housed in tropical biomes that nestle in a crater the size of 30 football pitches'. I was keen to visit, but it was situated about 3 miles off the main road, and I didn't have the time to spare as I had over 100 miles to cycle that day. So, I carried on towards Liskeard, Callington, and Tavistock, but promised myself I'll visit the Eden Project the next time I am in the area.

As I was totally unfamiliar with the area and hadn't really checked up on the easiest route, I basically just took the most direct route, but I am sure there must be easier ways to get to Exeter. I don't think I've ever cycled up and down so many hills in my life!

I remember cycling down one stretch of road which seemed to go on forever, on the other side of the valley I could see the road heading back up – and it was frightening. Somehow, I managed, and eventually reached Tavistock which is right on the edge of Dartmoor. There, I had to make a choice whether to head north on the A386 or travel slightly south towards Princetown and go right through the middle of Dartmoor.

This might sound strange, but I knew nothing of Dartmoor. In my head, I was thinking, *if it's a moor it's got to be flat*. I had visions of great, vast land set before me on the flat, with Exeter at the other side.

Boy, was I wrong! I went up and up and up, then down, then up again. When I stopped at Princetown, I was completely done in and really hoped Dartmoor would flatten at some point. I decided to stop at the local pub, The Prince of Wales, for something to eat.

After enjoying a great scampi and chips, along with two freezing cold pints of cider, I asked the landlord if the rest of my trip to Exeter would be flat across Dartmoor. He replied that he didn't know, because he wasn't from 'round these parts'.

When I asked where he lived, and he replied, 'Upstairs', I was beginning to think he was taking the piss a bit. However, I persevered.

'How long have you lived here?' I asked.

He replied, 'Just over two years.'

I tried another angle. 'Have you ever at any time in your life left this pub and visited Exeter?'

'Yes,' he said, 'but the wife drove, and she doesn't use the road through Dartmoor.'

The guy lives on the edge of Dartmoor for two years and not once has he thought, *I think I'll take a wander into Dartmoor and see what it's like.* Unbelievable!

I've no chance, I thought!

Then I reconsidered. I had 28 miles to go to Exeter. *How hard can it be? I can do 28 miles in a couple of hours.* So, I finished off my cider and headed full steam into the unknown of Dartmoor.

For about the next 12 miles or so, I was fine – (probably down to the effects of the cider) – but then I started to struggle, and other cyclists kept passing me. After an hour or so, I arrived at the Dartmoor Inn, where I came across a cycling event called the Milligan Charity Event.

When I stopped, most people thought I was part of the charity event, so I was given soup, bananas, energy bars, and drinks. I gratefully took the free handouts and took the opportunity to ask about the charity.

I was told that it had been set up after advertising executive Nick Milligan and his eight-year-old daughter, Emily, died in 2013 in a tragic family boat accident off the coast of Padstow in Cornwall. The pair had been thrown from their boat, and then run over by the out-of-control boat. It was a horrific story, and one I knew nothing about.

The Milligan Charitable Bike Ride involved 125 riders taking three days to cycle the 300-mile route from Trevose Golf Club in Cornwall to Trinity Fields in London. The money they raised was to be split between two charities: The Royal National Lifeboat Institution, and Child Bereavement UK.

After listening to the story, it brought home to me exactly why I was doing what I was doing, and it gave me the real boost I needed to get to Exeter. I was told I faced a 3-mile climb to reach the top of Dartmoor and then the cycling would get easier. So, I joined in at the back of some of the other riders, and their slipstream carried me to the top of Dartmoor where I stopped for a deserved photo at the carpark there.

I felt great again because I knew I didn't have far to go now, and it was a great ride from there. Joe phoned to say he had booked us into a nice hotel in Exeter, and he would be waiting on me for when I arrived.

I don't think I had ever been as pleased to see him. When I got to the van, I noticed he had got it lettered with *In memory of Ian Horne* and the dates of his birth and when he died. As a piss-take, he had given me a mention as well. On the back of the van it read, *WA Horne, outside taps supplied and fitted £40.* With me being a plumber, he thought it hilarious – and it was.

Then we noticed the dates he had put for Ian's death were wrong. He had put Ian's birthday 18th April instead of the 10th of June when he died. He was a bit embarrassed and then we played a bit of who was to blame game, but it was all in jest. However, I know Gary back at Bullet was already arranging to get it changed.

I had a shower at the hotel and went down for dinner. I think I had two pints of beer with my dinner and was so tired I almost fell asleep at the table. Time for bed.

I paid the bill and picked up a Help for Heroes wristband, which reminded me of one my best mates, Stuart Gilmour. I was planning to meet up with him in two days' time, as he and his wife Sara were going to join me from Bristol north-wards on Sunday for the day.

Land's End to Exeter, done.

14

*'We forget all too soon the things we thought
we could never forget.'*

Joan Didion, *American novelist*

Saturday, 21 June:

I got up early and checked a few messages and the donation page. We had set a £5000 target for the cycle, and already the donations had reached £3700. I had also received a message from David Moulsdale, Ian's friend from Optical Express, who said he was going to donate £1000 to the fund. So, I was confident that the target would be reached even before the first weekend was complete.

I was amazed at the generosity of some people, whether it was a £5 text or a donation like David's. To think people were watching this on Facebook and making donations was incredible.

Today I was heading from Exeter to Bristol, roughly 92 miles and a climb of about 2000ft. The previous day had been roughly 8000ft of a climb, so I expected today to be a walk in the park. I had been trying to explain to Joe just how hard cycling 8000ft was, and the easiest way I could describe it was by saying it's like cycling up Ben Nevis twice! Anyone who has climbed Ben Nevis will maybe have an idea of exactly what I mean.

It was a beautiful morning and the riding was great. It would be mainly B roads today taking me from Exeter to Cullompton, then on to Wellington and through to Taunton for lunch, before heading on to Bristol.

I stopped at Cullompton for a snack and a drink, and phoned home for a quick word with my wife, Mhairi, and the kids. It was really hot, and I remember buying an ice cream which I ate while talking to them. In fact, I managed to go back into the shop and buy another one and eat it while still talking to the family.

My next goal was Taunton – a place I had never been before, though I knew that it was famous for cider-making. It certainly took me by surprise how big it was, and had a beautiful town centre and castle. The place was buzzing, with music, street performers, acrobats, jugglers, and people on stilts, and there was some sort of festival going on in front of the Castle.

I loved it there, and the weather was roasting. I found a bar at the back of the square outside the castle, chained the bike up, then went inside and ordered food and a pint of Taunton Cider, I was so thirsty I just about downed it in one go, so I ordered another and sat outside in the scorching sunshine.

My food came and I sat and watched everything going on around me, soaking it all in and feeling really good.

I took out my phone and started checking messages and emails. Then I did something that had always come naturally to me – I clicked Ian's number on my phone, and dialled it to tell him about where I was and what I was up to.

I honestly don't know if it was the effects of the cider or not, but for a few seconds I genuinely forgot that Ian had died.

When I realised what I was doing, I switched the phone off and sat there for a minute or two in a daze, before being overwhelmed by feelings of guilt. Guilt that I had forgotten Ian was not with me anymore and I would never hear his voice again.

As I felt the tears coming, I managed to hide my distress from the people sitting across from me. As I pulled myself together, I convinced myself that it was the cider that had made me forget, and that I had no option but to finish my food and set off for Bristol.

My mood had switched dramatically from happiness to sadness, and Taunton didn't seem as appealing any more. Time to move on.

*

Joe had mentioned to me that he wanted to meet me and take me into Cheddar Gorge on my way to Bristol. It would mean a detour, but the plan was that he would meet me on the main road, take me into Cheddar Gorge for dinner, and then take me back out onto the main road again.

Not long after leaving Taunton, I passed through a village called North Petherton where all I could hear were church bells ringing. I stopped outside the church and asked a lady what was going on, and she explained that the sound was wedding bells and they were waiting on the bride and groom coming out of the church.

I stopped and put my bike against the church wall and waited on the happy couple coming out of church. When they emerged, followed by the wedding party, I took some pictures on my phone. Then for some crazy reason, while the wedding photographer was getting them to pose, I went straight up to them and asked if I could get a photo with the bride and groom. I think they were a wee bit shocked, but luckily enough I was wearing the Macmillan Cancer charity cycling top, and this touched them as the bride's father had passed away from this horrible disease and Macmillan had helped their family.

It's moments like that which made the charity ride so special.

Some weeks later, Rachel, the bride, and I exchanged a few messages on Facebook:

Rachel *It was a pleasure to meet you. Congratulations on your amazing contribution to such an amazing charity. Love from Mr and Mrs xx*

Pat *I have only just seen this post. And can I just say that it was an absolute pleasure to meet Allan Horne. It made my daughter Rachel and her husband Paul's day, to think he took the time to stop off and be a part of their special day. got some cracking photos. it holds really dear to Rachel because in the last two and a half years she has lost her dad. Grandad. and auntie to cancer, and the Macmillan nurses played a huge part in their lives. (Especially her dad). So, a big thankyou to Allan and keep up the good work. as the saying goes it was the icing on the cake x*

Allan Horne *Just looking through some pics of cycle n came across this. Lol. Sorry for Photobombing.... But thank you for being part of our incredible journey, in the end we raised 10k. Not bad for a week's work...*
The story of the wedding has had many a mention since, over a beer or 2 and looking back I'm not sure it was the PC thing to do after just walking out the church... It was a spur of the moment thing and thank you and again let me apologise.... Ps. I had a wee look at your FB wedding pics and they look amazing... I'm sure the one with me in it will be on your fireplace... Say hi and thank you to your Husband and have a lovely time together.... Allan

Rachel *Hi Allan, no worries for photobombing. It was a pleasure to be part of your Journey. Macmillan is a charity that's very close to my heart after I lost my Dad to cancer in 2011, so it was a pleasure to have you and the charity as part of our day. Unfortunately we don't have a fireplace, but the photo is in our wedding album so we can always look back and remember. The Hubby says hi back and a huge congratulations on the 10k you raised. And you never know, we may see you on your next journey if you're passing through... Rachel*

Things happen for a reason, and my sadness at calling Ian began to fade after seeing these two strangers getting hitched. I said my farewells and headed towards Cheddar Gorge, 25 miles away. From there, it would be only 18 more miles to Bristol, so I was already about halfway for that day.

About 8 miles south of where Joe was picking me up, I stopped at a garage for some water. Although I knew where I was going, and was using satellite navigation on my phone, I asked the guy behind the counter how far Cheddar Gorge was, and he told me about 25 to 30 miles. I had guessed in my head about 8 miles to meet Joe on the main road then approximately 4 or 5 miles' drive into the Gorge.

When I left the garage I was a bit confused by the guys estimate so I started checking the phone again and started to doubt myself, but I headed in the direction I thought I should be going. When I saw a sign for a village, I tried to look at my phone to find it while still on the bike, and my front wheel hit the kerb! I went flying one way while my phone went the other.

When I got up, I checked the bike was ok, and then saw that my phone was smashed to pieces. I could still use it, but the screen was all smashed and cracked; I also had blood coming from my shin.

I contacted Joe and it turned out I was exactly where I'd thought I was, and he was waiting for me just along the road. So, that was twice I'd asked locals for directions and twice they haven't had a clue where **they** were, never mind where I was going!

Eventually, I met Joe and we headed into the Cheddar Gorge – another place I had never been and knew nothing about. The place is stunning and reminded me of being in the French or Italian Alps. I am sure the great weather played a part in this, but the place is undoubtedly stunning.

I got Joe to stop the van for a little while, as there were rock climbers above us, and I wanted to watch their routes. I love rock climbing, and I made myself a promise that I would try and organise a climbing weekend down here in the near future.

Joe treated me to fish and chips in a great café in the Gorge, then he took me back onto the main road, the A38, which led straight into Bristol.

That night I was booked into another Travelodge, which was on the other side of the city at a retail park called Cribs Causeway. I was completely done in when I reached Bristol, which is another hilly town, and had to ask a few locals directions to Cribb's Causeway because my phone was out of charge.

One guy said, 'You don't want to go there.'

'Why?' I asked.

His friend replied, 'Because at this time of night all the shops are closed.'

Do I look like I am on a shopping trip? I thought to myself. All I wanted was a shower, some food, a few beers, and a bed, and here was a local thinking I'd come down from Glasgow on my bike to do some shopping!

As I headed from the main part of Bristol up to Cribs Causeway, I reckoned that the guys from Bullet had looked for a hotel at the top of a hill, as a piss-take! It's probably not even a steep hill, but after the day I'd had, I could have collapsed when I saw it.

The final straw was when I cycled past the hotel – not noticing Joe, who was actually shouting and waving at me to stop – and carried on into the huge retail park. I cycled round for ages looking for a Travelodge, scared to ask anyone directions in case they sent me away on another wild goose chase.

Eventually, I stopped a guy and asked if I could borrow his phone to contact Joe. When he answered, he explained that I had passed him, so I headed back and finally, thankfully, saw the hotel.

Another day of cycling done. Two days down, seven more to go.

It was a Saturday night, though, so I told Joe to get the beers in while I went for a quick shower and would be straight back out. I wanted to head into town to see what Bristol was like.

To be fair, my head was thinking of a night out in Bristol, but every part of my body was screaming 'Go to bed!' As usual, I never listened to myself, and got a taxi with Joe and headed into town.

We had a pint in a main street pub then came across The River Cottage Canteen, which is owned by the TV chef, Hugh Fearnley-Whittingstall. It's a fancy diner place, where we had a few overpriced beers, but decided not to eat there. Instead, we chose a kebab house across the road, and had a good laugh at what Hugh Fearnley-Whittingsall would have thought of someone leaving his posh eatery for a kebab shop. That's Scottish athletes for you!

As you can probably guess, I am not your average athlete or following an athlete's diet. I have always wondered what would have happened if I had eaten healthily while I was doing the cycle ride. I suppose I might have lost weight or felt fitter, but drinking and eating whatever I fancied never really affected my riding the next day.

I finally gave into my body and virtually collapsed into my bed. Tomorrow, I was going to be teaming up with my life-time friend, Stuart Gilmour, and his wife, Sara. Happy Days!

15

*'To have no heroes is to have no aspiration, to live on the
momentum of the past, to be thrown back upon routine.'*

Charles Horton Cooley, *American sociologist*

Sunday, 22nd June:

Today was going to be a great day for a few different
reasons.

- Hopefully, after today we would have reached our target
  of £5000 for our charity cycle.

- I would be meeting my lifetime friends, Stuart and Sara
  Gilmour.

- A good friend of mine and Ian's – Scott Cunningham
  MBE – would be taking part in the Commonwealth
  Games Queens Baton relay in the local village next to
  our home town, The Law Village.

Stuart Gilmour has been a friend of mine since schooldays
and I remember him telling me he was going to join the
Army when we were just teenagers. 'You will be home by
Christmas,' I told him.

But here we are, over 25 years later, and Stuart has reached
as high a rank as he can achieve. He has served his country all over the world, been on the ground in many war-torn
regions, and had recently been given an award for his work

in Afghanistan where he led a troop out there and returned without any fatalities under his watch. That was a rare occurrence, and something he was extremely proud of.

He has been married to Sara for over twenty years, and we teamed up a few years ago when we did a cycle ride through Spain together. So, I was really looking forward to teaming up with them again.

Scott Cunningham is a schoolfriend of mine from way back, but as the years went by, it was my brother Ian who became closer to Scott and helped him along the way. Scott contracted an incurable disease that affected his eyesight; he has now been blind for over 25 years.

In the old days, Scott became a bit of a hermit, as you would expect after becoming blind. He wouldn't leave the house, refused to go anywhere, and didn't want help. But Ian helped Scott with his first talking computer, which made a big difference to his life, and managed to get him out the house by taking him to rock concerts and festivals.

Scott then got himself his first guide dog... and the rest is history. From then, he has travelled the world with his companions by his side. He had the first blind dog to walk the West Highland Way in Scotland, and he climbed the highest mountain in Britain, Ben Nevis, with the aid of his dog. Scott has always said Ian played a massive part in bringing him from darkness back to light again with the help of his computers and dogs.

A great fundraiser for the Guide Dogs for the Blind charity, Scott has raised well over 350k for them over the years and was awarded his MBE a few years back for his contribution to the charity. It's something I know Ian was extremely proud of.

Ian and Scott have always been royalists, and are the only two guys I know that have actually met royalty. Ian met the

Queen Mum at an awards ceremony in St Paul's in London, where he was presented with his Queen's Badge from the Boys Brigade. But Scott got one up on him, when he was invited to the palace to collect his MBE!

I had spoken to Scott and asked if he would wear Ian's Queens Badge, alongside his MBE, while carrying the Queen's Baton for the Commonwealth Games, and he said he would be delighted.

So later that day, while I was cycling from Bristol to Wolverhampton, Scott would be walking through his home village, carrying the Commonwealth Baton, and proudly wearing his MBE and Ian's Queen's Badge. Nice one, Scott Cunningham MBE!

I was off to meet my friends Stuart and Sara Gilmour at the train station in Bristol. They had decided they would meet me there, then travel around 50 miles with me from Bristol to Tewksbury along the A38, basically hugging the M5. I would then carry on to Wolverhampton.

We would be passing through Gloucester, Tewksbury, and Worcester, before reaching Wolverhampton.

It was great meeting up with Stuart and Sara again, and the riding was really flat and enjoyable. All the little villages were nice to pass through, and time was flying by because I had such good company with me. Before we knew it, we had reached Gloucester – again, having never been there before, I wanted to go into the centre to see Gloucester Cathedral and hopefully grab a quick pint. Stuart and Sara had arranged to get a train home from Tewksbury, so I was always aware that we needed to watch our time. But we worked out we would have enough time to visit the centre and get a beer.

We headed straight for the Cathedral and got a few pictures, then we headed into the centre. I got stopped by the police for riding my bike in a pedestrian zone, but I had no idea this was even against the law! After speaking with the policeman and explaining about the fund-raising ride, he let me off and pointed us in the direction of a pub. The weather was great, and it was really nice sitting catching up with old mates; actually, it was a little surreal to think I was there with them.

We had only another ten or eleven miles to go to reach Tewksbury, so it was an easy sprint to arrive there in plenty of time for Stuart and Sara to catch their train. Joe joined up with this, and we had enough time for the four of us to enjoy a pleasant lunch.

I was sorry to wave goodbye to them, and for a laugh I climbed up on top of a huge horse that greets you on arrival to Tewksbury, and gave them a huge wave goodbye.

Later that day, Stuart added a post on Facebook:

> **Stuart Gilmour**: *What an absolute fantastic day today with my 'true' friend Allan Horne, I had a heavy heart when I said goodbye today and really felt that I should be cycling North with him on the rest of his journey. I have nothing but admiration for his determination in taking this challenge in memory of Ian and know he will finish with ease. For the remaining miles may the wind be at your back and the sun be in your face Respect.*

I still had just under 60 miles to go to reach Wolverhampton, and now I was on my own again.

The next 20 or so miles just flew by. I was probably a bit tipsy from the alcohol, and I was buzzing. I felt no pain or muscle cramps, and I rode really well passing the villages and towns of Worcester, Hartlebury, and Kinver, before heading into Wolverhampton.

Again, Bullet had booked me into a Travelodge on the

outskirts of the town, and again, just when I thought I had reached my destination, I discovered I had a few more miles and hills to climb! It was nice to finally see the hotel, and I phoned Joe to see where he was. This time, I just wanted to lie down for a while before heading to the Harvester pub next door for something to eat.

After Joe and I had enjoyed our dinner, I headed to bed. As usual, I could not sleep, so I started checking text messages and Facebook, and realised we were just shy of reaching our target of £5000. I could not believe it. The Bullet staff had not even started racing me yet, and here I was 300 miles completed, and nearly at the £5000 target!

Then I noticed the donations passing the £5000 mark, and when I saw who had donated the money to push it over the target, I couldn't help but shed a few tears.

Loads of people had donated all day, and I loved reading all the messages. I will be forever in their debt, and hope they all know it was for a great cause. But with just 24 minutes left of Sunday, Ian's kids, Sara and Sandy, had donated £44 to the fund – and THEY were the ones who had pushed it over the target.

Tomorrow (Monday), the challenge of me v Bullet would start, and I was already about 300 miles ahead of them.

Later that day I would be meeting another friend, Paul Craven, who was going to join me for my last 20 miles or so towards Preston.

Day three done, 300 miles covered, target already reached – time for bed. Tomorrow, Preston.

16

'True charity is the desire to be useful to others with no thought of recompense.'

Emanuel Swedenborg, *author*

Monday, 23rd June:

Facebook message 6.30am:

> *The Race begins today... At 8am, Bullet Express are going to start cycling in their office and try to catch me... I've been told I am just over 300 miles ahead of them... I've a long day today. Over 100 miles to Preston. The A49 is going to be my friend for most of it... My quads are killing me, and I can hardly walk but No mucking about now. (Well, maybe a wee bit)... The race is on.....*

My route today would take me through Whitechurch, Riverton, Warrington, Wigan, Standish, and Preston. I'd be meeting Paul Craven, who was joining me for my last 20 miles and staying with me overnight in Preston. I was looking forward to seeing him, and for him to help me get over the line.

As it turned out, I absolutely smashed today's ride. The wind was at my back, the riding was either flat or a slight incline, and it was one of the few days there were no climbs. After cycling for a few hours, I stopped to check my phone and Facebook, to see how Bullet were getting on in the race. I noticed they had done over 100 miles!

I also got a great text message saying that Braidhurst High School in Motherwell had heard about my race on Radio Clyde and were going to forward a cheque for £300. It was funny that out of all the schools in our area, it was Braidhurst High which had donated, as that was where my Dad had been brought up. Here is the message the school sent to David at Bullet Express:

Hi David

I heard your news article on Friday in relation to Allan Horne cycling from Land's End to John o' Groats in memory of his brother. I work at Braidhurst High School in Motherwell and we would like to make a donation of £300 to boost his fundraising. I am aware there is a just giving page, however because we are a school we need to send a cheque. Can you please provide me with information on who the cheque should be written out to? Good luck Allan & team…

Facebook Replies

Morag Sheather *Hi, I am Allan's cousin and a former pupil of BHS. I am serving with the Royal Military Police in Afghanistan and you have just made me cry! Well done Angela!*

Allan Horne *Thank you Angela. Xxxx*

Jocky John Brown *Going to a great cause well done everyone at Braidhurst High School*

Mhairi Horne *That's brilliant x*

Audrey Davidson *Excellent x*

George Allan *Great effort!*

Bridget Mackay *Brilliant! X*

Siobhán Devine *How generous x*

It's amazing how things touch people and how generous people out there can be. Reading the messages, I felt over-whelmed and very grateful that everyone was doing their bit.

I rode on a bit and was still thinking about the miles Bullet had recorded. I noticed it had gone up to 133, and this was before lunch. They had only been riding for 3 hours and they had pedalled 133 miles on a static fitness bike? That surely couldn't be right, so someone, somewhere, was counting something wrong.

As I cycled past Haydock Park Racecourse, I stopped for a picture and took the opportunity to phone David to see how they were getting on. To my surprise, he told me the reason their miles were so high was that they were counting train-ing runs which David and Gary had carried out the previous week in a bid to get fit for the challenge.

I couldn't believe it and I was laughing my head off at how competitive David and Gary were. But I refused to let them use their '110 training miles' and got them to reset the total to what it should be...

I had completed my cycle from Wolverhampton to Haydock in great time, and was feeling good. Joe and I met for lunch, and he explained that he would meet my friend Paul at Preston Travelodge, then Joe would bring him back to Wigan along with his bike so that he could join me for the last 20 miles of the day.

I reached Wigan way ahead of Paul and Joe, and so I just went to a pub beer garden along from the train station, sent Joe the address of the pub, and lay in the sunshine until they arrived.

This had been by far the best day for riding, and I felt good. All my aches and pains were gone and, to be honest, I hadn't even felt tired. I knew the next 20 miles to Preston with Paul would fly in, as it always does when you are in company.

It was great to see him. We've been friends since we met in 2007 in Kathmandu, Nepal, of all places, when we were both part of a group doing some climbing out there and visiting Everest Basecamp.

We became friends, and have since met up a few times a year, either climbing or for the odd weekend on the lash with the guys. We usually meet in the Lake District, where Paul has a second home, or down in Manchester, or sometimes Paul will venture north to meet us in the Highlands.

Paul had been the first to donate to the cycle when it was first announced, and he was the guy who – embarrassingly – Ian had to remind me who he was, back in the hospital. Thinking back, that was the last conversation I had with Ian.

Once he'd dropped Paul off, Joe was heading back to Preston as there was a possibility Bullet were going to change drivers. Joe was then going back up home for some work, and another driver, Bobby, was going to take over. He was not 100% sure what was happening, but said he would meet us at the Travelodge in Preston in a few hours and he would know by then.

As we made our way out of Wigan town centre, I could see Paul was a little nervous with all the traffic going past. He admitted he hadn't done much cycling recently, but it's amazing how quickly you just get used to the traffic. As soon as we were away from the town centre, he relaxed and we had a good laugh about things; the 20 or so miles just flew by.

We met Joe at the hotel, where he had already put all my gear up in the room. He had been brilliant at all that type of stuff throughout our trip, and I was embarrassed that he was doing it when I was perfectly able to do it myself. But that was Joe – he's an absolute gem.

Sadly, it turned out that his time with me was over and he would be heading back to Scotland, where he would do a van swap with his fellow driver, Bobby.

Just before Paul and I went out for some dinner, Bobby contacted me and said he would just catch up with us in the morning at breakfast.

It was a Monday night, we decided to go to an Italian restaurant first, then we headed to a few bars to try and watch one of the World Cup football matches on tv. But by the time we had eaten, the games were just about finished. When we asked a few people if there were any pubs with any kind of atmosphere, we were told that on a Monday there was only one pub that was busy, but it was a student-type bar which was full of kids about 18 to 20 years old.

Disappointed, we ended up just getting a few pints before heading back to the hotel. It was a bit of a shame, as both Paul and I had been expecting more of a night in Preston, but there was nothing else for it than to get to bed.

Tired, there was just time to reflect on another day down, and another hundred miles along the road. I had now travelled approximately 380 miles in 4 days; and Bullet had travelled 160 miles in one day (including training miles!).

Before I fell asleep, I checked my emails and Facebook, and realised we had just about reached £6000 in donations. I just could not believe it! Could we maybe reach the £10,000 mark? Surely not.

The next morning, I'd be leaving Paul in Preston and crossing over the border into Scotland. I was excited, but I knew there was a hell of a climb to overcome – from Kendal, south of the Lake District, up over the hill climb of Shap, then downhill to Penrith, and finally, north to Scotland.

I'd never cycled up over Shap but had been told it's a killer. We were about to find out!

17

'There is a magnet in your heart that will attract true friends. That magnet is unselfishness, thinking about others first; when you learn to live for others, they will live for you.'

Paramahansa Yogamanda, *Indian yogi and guru*

Tuesday, 24ᵗʰ June:

I got up out of bed early and headed for breakfast with Paul, and met Bobby for the first time. I had got used to Joe being with me, so it was strange to have a new companion, but we soon got chatting about my brother.

When Ian got married, Bullet had arranged for their hospitality carrier and driver to take him (and a nurse) from Monklands Hospital to the wedding reception at the Applebank Inn in Larkhall. It turned out that Bobby had volunteered to be the driver that night, and had even taken Ian back to the hospital later that evening. I was grateful for him taking his time out to do this, and was pleased to get the chance to thank him.

I introduced Paul to Bobby, and told him the story about Paul donating the money and me not realising it was him until Ian told me, 'It will be your friend Paul from Manchester.' Ian was always correcting me and, funnily enough, he was very rarely wrong. I can smile now from time to time thinking that even in his last breaths he was still correcting me. Not sure I should say I really miss that, but I do, and always will.

After breakfast, we said goodbye to Paul and my plan for the day was to ride from Preston to Lancaster, Kendal, up over Shap, Penrith, and over the border to Lockerbie. This was going to be one of the longest days on the bike, but I felt up for it and could not wait to get my Scotland flag out when I reached Gretna.

I followed the A6 mainly all the way to Kendal via Lancaster, where I stopped for a snack. Lancaster is another place we pass all the time heading south but have never actually stopped at. It's a lovely place with a really nice town centre, with small streets going off in all directions from the main area. I found a nice café and had some food, then set off to meet Bobby in Kendal for lunch.

Bobby picked me up in the centre of Kendal, and we drove around trying to find a quiet little pub or café for something to eat. We ended up at a fish and chip shop where I had a great fish supper and a few cans of coke. Like I said earlier, I am no athlete, so no need for nuts and raisins. I knew Shap was next, and I knew I had to get a good meal and rehydrate before setting off. Bobby said he would head up towards Shap and wait on me there.

As I started climbing, I could see the van parked in a layby further up the road. When I got to the van, Bobby was fast asleep in the driver's seat, so I did what anyone would do – I took a few photos of him sleeping, posted them on Facebook, and left him in peace.

The climb to the top of Shap was nowhere near as hard as I'd imagined and I was soon at the top, where there is a roadside marker to say you have reached the summit. I took a pretty bad selfie and posted it on Facebook, then my phone rang. It was Bobby to ask if I was ok, and he wondered if I'd passed without him noticing. I explained that I'd left him sleeping and was already at the top of Shap, so he came up to meet me and we had a good laugh about it.

We agreed we'd meet up again at Penrith, and I headed off shouting, 'It's all downhill from here!'

I thought I would be able to bomb it down the other side, but the wind was heading south into my face and it was freezing. I think the top speed I managed going downhill was about 32mph, which was a bit disappointing.

It was a good ride into first Penrith then down towards Carlisle, where I stopped for some drink and some food, but the minute I came off the bike I felt really dizzy and nauseous. To make matters worse, I dropped my sunglasses in front of me, then ran over them just as I was stopping.

I went into a service station and bought some water, crisps, and a Mars bar, which I ate and drank, then set off again. I knew I had about another 25 miles to go, and probably about 2 hours cycling ahead of me.

I must have cycled for about 10 of those miles when I suddenly felt really sick. I pulled over and threw up, then sat for a bit and just lay down. I could have slept there and then, no sleeping bag, no covers nothing I just wanted to curl up and sleep. Bobby pulled over in the van and gave me some water, and I took a few headache pills. I also filled my water with a high energy powder sachet, then headed off to reach Gretna.

Bobby was waiting for me at the Gretna sign, and I got some great photos of me with my Scotland flag and my Macmillan Cycle shirt on.

I look happy in the photos. Inside I was feeling lousy, but it felt great to be back in Scotland. Psychologically, it was the halfway mark in my cycle, and I knew the next day I would actually be passing through my home town, Larkhall, which was a great boost. We headed off for Lockerbie and onto Lochmaben, where I was staying that night.

When I got to the hotel, one of my friends, Derrick Jones, had come down to visit me for the night. Derrick has been a mate for many years, and it was great to see him. I was totally done in and went straight for a shower, then lay on the bed for a while to check my messages. I noticed that the fund had gone way beyond the £6000 mark and, along with the cheque from Braidhurst High and other cash donations, we had so far raised over £7000.

I hadn't really kept in touch with Bullet that day, but noticed that I had now travelled 485 miles in what was my fifth day; Bullet in the office were just 200 miles behind on their static bike, so they were catching me up.

I noticed during the cycle even when my body felt tired, I found it really hard to sleep, your body feels completely done in and you can hardly move but my mind was always racing when I finished for the day and it took forever to relax and drift off so I wasn't saying no when Derrick suggested a pub crawl of Lochmaben. There are only a few bars in Lochmaben, and we went into one which Ian and I visited just two years before.

That made me laugh because on that occasion, Ian had gone outside for something and somehow found a penguin suit in a bag. I can only guess that someone had thrown it out, but Ian put it on and ran back into the pub shouting, 'You don't want to go out there, it's fucking freezing!' Everyone in the pub had a good laugh about it, and for the rest of the night the barmaid kept asking Ian for ice. I still laugh thinking about it now.

Derrick and I went back to the hotel and sat out the back with a couple of beers until 2am. So much for me feeling sick and tired! Looking back, I still don't know how I managed to get up each morning and do what I did.

That was Day 5 out the way. The next day I would be joined by two of Bullet's friends to head up into my local town, then over to Bullet's offices for lunch, and finishing up at the Drovers hotel in the village of Ardlui at Loch Lomond. It would be 126 miles in one day, but there would be two cyclists helping me and knew that once I got past Abington, the riding would be pretty flat all the way.

18

'I think togetherness is a very important ingredient in life,
some have the correct ingredients but wrong method, but
when all mixed up they should always remain together.'
Barbara Bush, *former First Lady of the USA*

Wednesday, 25th June:

Although I went to bed late, I got up really early, about 6am, and decided to get out and clean my bike. Bobby had left me all my tools and cleaning gear for sorting the bike. His house was only about an hour away, so he had decided to head home last night and this morning he was bringing down two riders to join me – Frazer Ferguson and Ross Harris.

Frazer had known Ian for a while, and only recently I found out that he had actually played football with Ian and me ten years previously in the charity match at Ibrox Stadium, home of our team Glasgow Rangers.

Frazer was a part-time cyclist – a bit like myself – and he was going to cycle up with me to Bullet's offices in Bothwell. Ross, on the other hand was going to ride all the way to our destination that day, 126miles away at the Drovers Hotel on the banks of Loch Lomond, he was a really good cyclist. I was told he had done really well in the previous Etape Caledonia race, which is an 80-mile road race in Pitlochry Perthshire. I had entered the race myself the previous year, but had been happy enough just to finish it, never mind do well.

We had breakfast along with Bobby and Derrick, then said our goodbyes and set off.

There is a back road from Lochmaben that brings you out at the Dumfries and Moffatt roundabout, so that was the route we took, and from there we headed along the old A74 to Abington. I tucked in behind Ross and Frazer, and it was great riding with them. They were cutting out the wind for me, and I was just getting sucked along in the slipstream. It was really the first time on the trip I had noticed the difference of riding in a group.

We stopped at Abington for a drink and a snack, and I looked at our times. We were absolutely flying along, and I knew from here to Larkhall and Bullet's offices, then onto Loch Lomond, was going to be mainly flat.

I phoned my mum and told her to expect us to pop in for a cup of tea. We battered along the road, and in no time we were at the top of my home town of Larkhall. The kids were in school and unfortunately my wife Mhairi was working, but we had all arranged to meet at The Drovers Hotel that night, so I knew I would see them all in a few hours.

It was a bit bizarre cycling through Larkhall. A few people nodded but they would probably have had no idea where we had just cycled from. We stopped at my mum's house and, as usual, she had gone to town and bought loads of pies, sausage rolls, and cakes. But we had arranged to have lunch when we got to Bullet's offices, so we had a quick cup of tea and a snack with my mum and headed off.

On the way to Bothwell, we cycled through the town of Hamilton. I was heading down to a set of traffic lights, which were at red, when I noticed the guy in a car a few in front looking in his mirror and watching me move down the inside next to the kerb. He started slowly moving his car towards the kerb to block me off and I nearly came off my bike as I was clipped into the pedals. I got past him, but Ross and Frazer didn't.

The next thing I knew, Frazer was round the car at the driver's window and giving him verbals. I was just waiting on the lights turning green, so it took me a second or two to realise what was happening. Frazer had hardly said a word for about fifty miles, and now he had just turned into Ronnie Kray! Ross and I just looked at each other laughing. Little, quiet Frazer.

We arrived at Bullet's offices and it was great to see all the staff out cheering us. We also saw some friends who were going to join us to cycle up to The Drovers Hotel at Loch Lomond. David and Gary were coming, along with Dave Freeland from my local hillwalking club, and David Maguire who was an old neighbour but also a friend of Ian's from the Go Karting and Mini Moto biking with Sandy.

We had a great lunch and I got some photos with the office staff on their static bike. We compared miles and at this point I had done 640 miles, while Bullet had done 525 miles. They were catching up, but I was still in front!

When I looked at the running total in the MacMillan fund, it had nearly reached £7000! Absolutely unbelievable.

After lunch, we set off, and it struck me for first time that I had no idea what route to take with everyone. Dave Freeland suggested we take the cycle path route, the NCN7 route, from Glasgow Green to Balloch on the banks of Loch Lomond. There were all kinds of bikes – mountain bikes, hybrid, and road bikes – which was brilliant. Unfortunately, for the very first time on my trip, the rain started.

It poured all the way, but it didn't dampen our spirits. It was great fun riding with everyone, and the cycle route was brilliant, taking us places along the River Clyde that I hadn't even known existed.

By the time we got to Balloch, we split up a bit and Ross and I headed off along the road. While the cycle path is good, you can't get real speed up and it can be quite dangerous on a road bike. So, Ross and I pushed on and arranged to have the beers ready at The Drovers Hotel.

Ross gave me a high five and told me it was the first time in his life he had cycled more than 100 miles in one day. I was quite proud that I was with him when he achieved this, because he is a really good and keen cyclist.

We saw the Bullet support van in a layby up ahead, and cycled up to find Bobby sleeping again. This time, I woke him and told him the others were on their way. It is a really tricky, narrow road along the Lochside, so I just said to head up to the Drovers and we would be there in half an hour.

As we turned at Tarbet along the A82, one of my mates, Sandy Waddell, pulled his car over to us. Also in the car was my wife Mhairi, our two kids Alex and Sacha. It was great to see them, but it is quite a narrow road and a dangerous place to stop. So, I quickly said hello and that we would get them in the Drovers shortly.

We arrived at the Drovers and I was buzzing to see everyone. The amount of family and friends who had come along was unbelievable and soon the rest of the cyclists arrived. We all sat down for some dinners and beers, and I realised I was as dirty as I have ever been in my life. It had been raining all the way from Bothwell, and all the spray had completely covered me.

I also noticed Peter Cornfield and Rose Quinn in the pub. They are friends from the hillwalking club who told me they were going to join me for the next day or two. Rose planned to drive Peter's car along the route so Peter could cycle with me and then he could get a lift back home.

The night in the Drovers was brilliant. Ian's wife Jean and the two kids, Sara and Sandy, joined us. And my cousin John Brown also popped in, which was great, as I had been keeping in touch with him all along the way from Land's End.

We had some great laughs, but unfortunately the road was being closed at 10pm for roadworks on the A82, so everyone had to leave to head home at 9.30pm. I was sorry to see them all go, but the adrenalin was wearing off and my body was going into shutdown mode. Another day done!

I went across to my accommodation for the night and found the room had a big four-poster bed. Forgetting how dirty I was, I just lay down for a minute before I was going to get a shower. But this time I was so tired, I just couldn't get back up, and ended up crashing out until I woke the next morning at six o'clock!

When I got up and looked at the bed, it was completely filthy. You would have thought a coalman had been sleeping in it!

Sorry, Drovers. A bit embarrassed, I showered and got ready for my new day. I'd be setting off from Ardlui and travelling about 85 miles north, to Invergarry. This stretch hopefully should be a bit easier.

19

'There is no glory in climbing a mountain if all you want to do is get to the top, it's experiencing the climb itself, in all its moments of revelation, heartbreak, and fatigue. That is the real goal.'

Karyn Kusama, *American film and TV director*

Thursday, 26th June:

Our ride today is only 85 miles. Last night I said goodbye to Bobby, as he had to head back to Bothwell, and one of Bullet's owners Gary Smith was taking over from him and joining us later in the day. I'd enjoyed having Bobby along and, like Joe before him, I was sad to see him go.

Today I was being joined by Peter Cornfield and Rose Quinn – friends from Blantyre Hill Walking Club. Peter was going to cycle with me while Rose was driving his car in front. Our plan was that Peter would stay up at Invergarry Bunkhouse and come home with Rose the next day.

The route, which I had travelled many times before, would take me up into Glencoe, on to Fort William, and along over the Commando Monument and down into Invergarry.

The rain had dried up overnight and the cycling was good, with Peter leading the way. I always think the A82 is a dangerous road for cycling, but it is not nearly as busy as you would imagine with it being the main road from Glasgow to Fort William.

We had just passed the town of Crianlarich when Peter swerved to the side to miss a pothole and I then smacked straight into it. My first puncture of the trip! Luckily, I had a spare inner tube, because the support van was 90 miles away at Bullet's offices in Bothwell. I had to laugh: the first time I'd needed the support crew and they were 90 miles away. Jokingly, I text David and Gary to complain about lack of support, so to be fair, David stopped the static bike riding in the offices for half an hour while I fixed my puncture.

Back on the road again, we cycled past The Bridge of Orchy Hotel and up onto Rannoch Summit on Rannoch Moor, then down into Glencoe. I had a look up at Buachaille Etive Mor and Curved Ridge route on the mountain, and immediately thought of the climb I had done with Ian, when we mistimed the climb and had to dig a snow-hole for the night. When we looked back on it later, although we could have frozen to death, we actually enjoyed the night up there and always joked about it. Ian always wound me up about not having any food left that night and his midget gem sweets he shared with me saved my life from starving to death. My toes got frozen up there, and even to this day I still get pins and needles on the tips of my toes. It's always a reminder of my climbing up there with Ian.

Cycling through Glencoe you have the Aonach Eagach ridge on your right-hand side, which is another ridge I climbed over with Ian. And at the end of the ridge you have the Clachaig Gully. I remember a time with Ian when we asked a guy at the summit cairn which was the best way down off the ridge. The guy told us to follow the path towards the Pap of Glencoe and we would see the path leading easily down to the road. Or, he warned, we could go down the Clachaig Gully route but it's very steep and dangerous and a few people have died going down it. Of course, for Ian it was a no-brainer: we were going down the Clachaig Gully route. Thankfully, we lived to tell the tale.

On the left of Glencoe, you pass the little Buachaille then the hidden valley, where the infamous massacre of Glencoe took place, then further up there's a climb into a broad gully on Coire nan Lochan, with Bidean Nam Bien behind, which leads across the top and back down to the Clachaig Hotel.

I've climbed them all at various times with Ian or with friends. But in most cases, I climbed them first with Ian, then went with friends at a later date.

I love Glencoe. It's one of Scotland's most beautiful places, no matter what the weather is like. If it's sunny, the scenery looks amazing; if it's dark and rainy, the place looks mysterious and eerie; if covered in snow, its appearance is second to none. No matter the weather, it's just dramatic and atmospheric every time you pass through.

We had arranged to stop at Fort William, so we pressed on with Peter in front and me tucked in behind. I was using him for as much slipstream as I could manage.

Gary overtook us in the van and pressed the horn repeatedly as he passed, giving me the fright of my life! I told him so, in slightly more colourful terms, when we caught up with him at Morrison's supermarket car park in Fort William. There, we put our bikes in the van and headed up to the Ben Nevis Inn at the foot of Ben Nevis. This is where the tourist path leads up to the summit of Ben Nevis, albeit it's about 4000+ft above you.

The food in the pub is great. I've eaten there loads of times and never had a bad meal. After a lovely lunch with Peter, Gary, and Rose, Gary dropped us off at the roadside with our bikes and we set off for Invergarry Bunkhouse. He was going on ahead to get the accommodation sorted for us.

I thought Gary had never stayed at a bunkhouse before, and I didn't know what he was expecting. Bunkhouses are pretty much what it says on the tin – you get a house with bunk accommodation, usually 2 bunks upwards in a room, and you share the room with whoever has booked in that night. Before he set off, I asked him to go to the shops and get some pizza, beers, and some snacks for the night.

It's an easy ride from Fort William to Spean Bridge, but just as you get out of Fort William, you come through Torlundy. Torlundy is where Ian used to help out as a fishing ghillie on the Camisky Estate. It looks up into the North Face of Ben Nevis, and again this is a place that has given me so many great memories. I must have climbed Ben Nevis about 15 times but have never actually walked up the tourist path.

The first time I climbed it was with Ian, from the North Face, where we hired a guide to take us up Tower Ridge in winter. I'll be honest and say that at that particular time we were probably both out our depth, because it's a grade 5 winter alpine climb. But we managed it, and although it was dark coming down, I can still remember exactly how shattered I felt.

I stopped briefly at the Torlundy sign and had a look up at the Ben, and thought back to some of the climbs we had done there.

Next it was down into Spean Bridge. There is quite a climb up to the famous Commando Monument from Spean Bridge – probably just over one mile uphill – but when you reach the top, you see the Commando Monument and the view along the Spean Valley towards the peaks of Ben Nevis and Aonach Mor.

The location of the monument was apparently chosen because it is on the route from Spean Bridge railway station to the former Commando Training Centre at nearby Achnacarry Castle. Prospective Commandos would arrive at the station after a 14-hour journey, load their kit bags onto waiting trucks, and then speed-march the 7 miles (11km) to the training centre in full kit with weapons, weighing a total of 36 pounds (16 kg). Anyone not completing the march within 60 minutes was immediately returned to their unit.

This famous landmark was another which brought back memories of Ian. One of the last photographs we had taken together was there, sitting with our cousin John Brown, after completing our climb of the Inaccessible Pinnacle on the Isle of Skye.

I stopped, along with Peter and Rose, and they took a few photos of me at the monument. But I was conscious that there were definitely two people missing that I would have wanted in the photo.

From there, we headed on along the A82, down through the woods, and onto the main road along Loch Lochy. The wind was battering towards us, but Peter was just in front, and again I tucked in behind him to get his slipstream.

As we were cycling past the loch near the little village of Laggan, Gary came cycling towards us. He had parked the van at the bunkhouse and cycled back to meet us. I asked if he had sorted the accommodation, and he just laughed and said, 'Well, yeah, we have a bed.' I had a wee laugh to myself as I reckoned Gary wasn't looking forward to the night in the bunkhouse.

I had stayed there before with my climbing club, so I knew what I was going to. The last time I had been there, I noticed there were paintings on the wall which were for sale. I might be wrong, but I think the guy who runs the place is an artist. There was one painting in particular that I had fancied buying, called Tower Ridge. It was basically a painting of Tower Ridge on Ben Nevis, and at the top there was a climber looking down. He was just himself. When I enquired about buying it, the owner was looking for £150, which at that particular time I thought was a bit pricey.

As we were cycling towards the bunkhouse, I had a wee thought that if the painting was still there, I would buy it this time.

We all arrived safely at the bunkhouse and Peter mentioned that the cycle we had just completed was 86 miles – the longest he had ever cycled.

We were in different dorms. Rose and Peter were in one dorm, while Gary and I were sharing another dorm with a couple of other guys. I was still thinking this was all new to Gary, but he said he had stayed at the bunkhouse at Bridge of Orchy before.

I noticed the Tower Ridge painting was still on the wall, and asked the guy how much he wanted for it. Obviously, he did not know I had been there before, so he asked me to make him an offer. I said I had no idea how much paintings cost, but would he accept £50? He shook his head and said he was looking for £150.

'Why don't we meet in the middle then?' I suggested. 'I'll give you £100 for it.'

He agreed, and the deal was done. To be honest, I would have happily paid £150 this time, but he seemed delighted with the £100. It now hangs in my dining room, where I've renamed it, 'Climbing Solo'.

Once we were settled, we stuck the pizzas on, had a few beers, and got talking to a few of the guests in the lounge area, or TV room. There were a couple from Spain who were doing a bit of travelling; a motor biker guy who was doing a tour of the Scotland NC500 and recording it all for a bike magazine; and a couple of Scottish hill walkers.

I checked my messages and I text David to see if we had any more donations. He confirmed we had now raised over £7000! I keep going on about it, but it was just overwhelming looking at the donations. I had never done anything like this before.

I also discovered a message from John Smeaton, wishing me luck on my trip.

John Smeaton was the baggage handler who became known around the world when he helped to prevent terrorists attacking Glasgow Airport back in June 2007. When asked live on Sky TV if he had a message for the terrorists, he famously said, 'Aye, Glasgow doesn't accept this, we will just set about ye. If any more extremists are still wanting to rise up and start trouble, know this: We'll rise right back up against you. New York, Madrid, London, Paisley... we're all in this together and make no mistake, none of us will hold back from putting the boot in.'

It was brilliant getting a message from him, as he now lives in New York and had messaged me through the Facebook pages.

I sent him a wee message back as well.

Looking back on that day's section, it had been fairly straightforward. I had completed over 100miles in each of the last two days. That was over 700 miles done, and when I checked how Bullet were getting on, they had reached 688 miles. So, I was still a few miles ahead, with two days left.

I now had roughly 170 miles left to get to John o' Groats. As the next day was a Friday, David was hopeful the fund total would go up because it would be wages day. He was hoping to reach the £10,000 mark, which was quite a lot in a couple of days... but fingers crossed.

Time for bed. Actually, for me, it was a couch. I hadn't told Gary this, but I hate bunkhouses and sleeping in dorms, so I just got my quilt and slept on the couch.

20

'Dining out with fine food and fine wine is wasted if you do not have a fine friend to dine with, luckily I had all three.'

AH, *HRH Flamingo 89109*

Friday, 27th June:

This was going to be my second last day on the bike, and from here onwards, I had no idea where I was going. I'd never been on the road from Invergarry towards John o' Groats, so studied the map and discovered that today's route was heading for Dornoch.

Peter and Rose had decided they would continue with us for part of the day, until we reached Dingwall, then they would head back down the road. I was delighted to have company on the road again.

The plan was to pass through Fort Augustus, on to Drumnadrochit, then towards Dingwall, and finishing at Dornoch. The weather was now a lot colder than when I'd started the challenge at Land's End, so instead of stopping for the odd pint here and there, I found myself stopping for a hot chocolate or some soup.

We cycled along the A82 – still the same road I had been on all the way from Glasgow – and just after we went through Fort Augustus, we got our first view of Loch Ness. The wind was coming off the loch and it was pretty cold. The roads were good, and it was reasonably flat along the banks of Loch Ness, but the traffic along this part was quite busy and it was not the most enjoyable part of the cycle. We started to climb, and I noticed a castle on my right, down towards the loch. It was Urquhart Castle, which I had seen some pictures of before but had never seen it in real life. I never stopped to visit it, purely because I was cold and hungry and food at Drumnadrochit was only a few miles away, but I've promised myself I'll come back and visit it another day.

When we arrived in Drumnadrochit, Rose and Gary were waiting on us and we headed over to one of the touristy cafes, where you can buy a cup of tea and a scone for about £15. I hate these wee tourist spots as they are just a rip-off. I think we ordered some soup, a drink, and a scone with butter.

I had a look at some souvenir Loch Ness monster whisky glasses that were on display, and picked up a couple of the souvenir Scottish marmalade jars, which I put on the table to buy along with the whisky glasses on our way out. When I turned round, Rose had the marmalade open and was spreading it on her scone. She thought it came with the scones! I was laughing my head off, as they cost about £6 each.

When you leave Drumnadrochit, there are two routes you can take: either to head for Inverness and on to Dingwall; or head for Beauly then on to Dingwall. We decided on the Beauly route, mainly because it came inland, away from the main road. What I did not know, though, was that I was about to have to cycle up one of the steepest hills in the whole trip. If I'd thought Devon and Cornwall were bad, this hill was a nightmare! The Culnakirk Climb, it's called – a 1-in-6 climb for over a mile.

I must admit Peter handled it better than I did. I stopped a few times and when I eventually got to the top, Peter was waiting. He said he had climbed the whole way without stopping, but I'm not ashamed to admit I didn't.

The beauty of this climb, though, was that after getting to its top we had a great run down the valley into Beauly, then we just kept going all the way into Dingwall. We had arranged to meet Gary and Rose there for lunch, then Peter and Rose would say their goodbyes and head back to Glasgow.

We found a pub down near the railway station and headed for a table. I came up with a plan about my four souvenir Loch Ness Monster glasses, and made up some silly story about me visiting a glass factory in a small village that never even existed, and pretended they were limited editions, worth £150 each. I then took a picture of them next to a malt whisky bottle, along with a picture of the box they came in, and posted it on Facebook offering them to the first person to donate £50 to the fund and post the words 'You're the best, Allan. Go, Go, Go.'

Within minutes, David McCutcheon had bought them, and we all had a good laugh about it. But to be honest, I would pay £50 to get them back, as I would love to have them as souvenirs of my journey. It was for a great cause, though, and thank you, David, for donating and helping me with a bit of fun along the way.

After lunch, Rose and Peter headed off with our thanks and best wishes, and it was now going to be just me and Gary all the way to John O Groats.

I only had 30 miles left to Dornoch. My ankle was giving me a little concern and the top of my foot was in pain – and, of course, my ass – but 30 miles could be done in two hours if I got some wind behind me and some flat riding. To be honest, it took me nearly three hours, and I was about 5 miles from Dornoch when Gary came back in the van. Earlier, he had said he would go up ahead and get us another bunkhouse for the night, so I thought maybe he was enjoying bunkhouses after all.

But when he met up with me, he was keen to tell me we would not be staying in a bunkhouse tonight. Instead, he had booked us into the Royal Dornoch Castle Hotel.

I admit to having been a little ignorant about Dornoch, and it wasn't until later that I found out they play golf there, and the Royal Dornoch Castle Hotel is a very fine hotel. Gary is one of the most down-to-earth guys I have ever come across, but I am sure he prefers this type of place to the bunkhouse. I was certainly delighted to be staying there.

As we were packing my bike into the van outside the hotel, Gary showed me his new Lycra cycling shorts and announced that he would be joining me for about 20 miles the next day, and would finish with me at John o' Groats. 'Gary, they look lovely, mate, now can you put the shorts back in the van and let's get into this hotel. I'm starving and freezing.

I actually felt a bit out sorts wearing all my cycling gear in the posh whisky bar, and I attracted a few looks, but I cared not a jot. I'm not a whisky drinker. I don't even like it, which is probably sacrilege coming from Scotland, but I don't really like spirits at all. So I just ordered a couple of pints and took some time to relax.

Gary said he had booked us for dinner at 8pm. I had no smart clothes with me, so I would just have to do with my cleanest t-shirt, jeans, and trainers.

I chose steak, which just cut into thin slices, and I must admit, it was without doubt the nicest meal I'd eaten on the whole trip.

At this stage of the journey, I had got used to the miles and wasn't as tired at the end of the daily rides any more. Also, the adrenalin was starting to kick in that I would be finishing this challenge the next day, after starting it not eight days earlier but nearly a year ago on the 17th September, 2013.

I was sore, and my body hurt when I moved. My ankle was a bit of a concern, and one of my cleats on the bike was broken, which was pointing my foot in a different position than usual, causing a spasm in my foot. I know most people would say just change it, but for some reason – and to be honest, I don't know why – I just wanted to finish with the bike I started with, and with nothing done to it apart from fixing the punctures.

After dinner, we headed down the road a bit to a more casual bar, and got talking to a group at the table next to us. I mentioned to one of the women in the group that most of the guys in the pub were dressed like golfers, with their pullovers and polo shirts. 'Is there a golf course about here somewhere?' I asked.

She asked if I was taking the piss – even Gary probably thought I was – but I genuinely had no idea that Royal Dornoch is one of the most famous golf courses in Scotland, and we were staying at that hotel. Gary described it as me staying at Gleneagles Hotel and not knowing there is a golf course there. But I've been to Gleneagles, and I do know they play golf there.

I wanted to go back to the hotel to check my messages and Facebook to see if we'd received any more donations, and to find out how far Bullet's staff were getting along on their static bike. This was their last day, and I was keen to know how they were going to finish.

It turned out that I was 80 miles away from John o' Groats and Bullet were 40 miles from completing their ride. So, David and Gary decided they would cycle 20 miles each to finish the miles for Bullet Express. David was in Spain, where he has a holiday home near where my family go each year in Murcia. He planned to cycle to the local pub I drink in out there which was approximately 20 miles from his Spanish home, while Gary was going to John o' Groats in the van, then cycle 10 miles back from there and join me for that last 10 miles back into John o' Groats. That way, we would all complete the same number of miles and we would all finish together.

When I checked some emails, texts and Facebook that night, I realised that our total was now close to £8000. And Gary reckoned that with cash & cheques still to come, we would probably be closer to £9000.

Could we pass the £10,000 mark in just over a week of cycling? I wondered. I really hoped so, but you can only go to the well so many times and I was sure everyone would be getting sick of the sight of us on Facebook. However, we could only hope. Certainly, I'd discovered all week that people everywhere relate to cancer. No-one really likes to talk about it, and obviously no-one wants to have it, but I don't think I had met anyone on my travels that had not been touched or affected by cancer in their lives.

I have no problem talking about Ian to people. I believe he changed lives for the better for most people he met. He was infectious and, yes, he had faults – we all do – but I don't think I or anyone could have had a better big brother than him.

People say time is a great healer, but in my opinion it's not. Ian was a huge mass in my life and now I have a huge void. You get on with things and you laugh, but many, many days and nights you cry – maybe not in front of people, maybe when you are alone in bed, maybe you're driving or out walking.

But I am sure it's the same the world over – you never really heal. It's the downside to having true, unconditional love for someone, but it's something I am getting on with and trying to manage the best I can.

During his illness, I saw courage and strength in Ian that I had never really seen before, and that is something I will always be proud of. I watched my dad go through it with pride and dignity and with no fuss, and I watched Ian do the same. I can only hope that when my turn comes around, I will face it with the same conviction that Ian and my dad had.

As I said at the start of this book, they were, and still are, my heroes.

Time for bed. That was my second last day over, and my end goal was finally in sight.

21

*'Be yourself, above all. Let who you are, what you are,
what you believe in shine through every day and with every
sentence you write, show every piece of you to the finish.'*

John Jakes, *American writer*

Final Day: Saturday, 29th June:

I got up with a little bit of a hangover and had breakfast with Gary. I only had 80 miles to go, but the woman from the bar last night had warned me about a few hills and described it as probably the hardest cycling I would do on my trip.

I think I told her I did not care, it would be easy, and that I was prepared for anything. But I was way wrong. I would admit, the section between Dornoch and John o' Groats probably was the hardest cycling I did on trip. I had looked at it on the computer and noted that it was only 3000ft of a climb, but it was the fierceness of the hills that killed me.

Gary said he would catch up in a little while, so I set off following the A9 to Brora (16 miles away) and arranged to stop there to meet him. And from there I'd head to Wick and finish at John o' Groats.

There's not much happening in that part of the world, although some of the views are stunning as it is a hilly coastal route. As you cycle along, you get to see the sea cliffs and the roads away in front of you, but it was windy and cold and I was pedalling into a strong headwind and I could hardly get any speed going. It was bad enough climbing the hills on the bike without the wind constantly battering against your face. A few times I wondered how David was getting on in Spain in the nice sunshine.

Eventually, I reached Brora and met Gary, who gave me some snack. He had decided he was going to auction his bike on Facebook, and donate the proceeds to our charity. It was a tremendous offer, as the bike was brand new. We took some pictures of the bike for the Facebook page then I set off again.

The next scheduled stop was going to be Berriedale. When you cycle along this route, it can be quite tiresome because you don't really see anyone. It's rolling hills and you get to a top and then there are dips all along. To be honest, I felt it quite a boring bit of road to be on, but after a while you get to see the cliffs and it looks like the edge of the world! You can virtually see the top of Scotland turning left, and you know you are heading for the top with nowhere to go and nothing there. Land's End is still a busy place with loads of little villages, but there is not a lot happening up at that end of our kingdom.

Just before I was to go down and up the Berriedale Braes, Gary drove back to warn me about them. I cycled down them, and usually I like a downhill, but this time I was too worried about having to get back up the other side. I could see Gary slowing down in the van and watching me begin the horrible cycle uphill.

My body was saying no but my head and heart were saying yes, so I just went down the gears and kept pedalling and pedalling until I thought I was at the top. I stopped for a rest and a drink, and was looking at my surroundings when I spotted a church graveyard behind me – It was Berriedale

Church and there was a grave with my surname on it! Horne is not the most common name, especially when it's spelled with an E on the end. But here I was staring at a grave of a Robert Horne who had died this very week 66 years before!! I don't deny it freaked me out a bit and I got goosebumps all over.

I found out later Berriedale Church was actually built and donated by landowner James Horne as far back as 1826. He was no relation, but the name Horne appears on over a dozen graves in the church graveyard. Still gives me goosebumps thinking of it now!

I set off again and found Gary was waiting along the road a bit. He said there was a café just 5 miles along the road, so we would meet there for some food. I asked him if he could just ride the van in front of me to try and keep the wind off me, but it didn't really help. The wind was coming in off the sea in a westerly direction, so it was hitting me side-on. Eventually, I told him just to head off and I would meet him at the café; I knew I wouldn't miss it, as there was not much else around.

Just before Gary sped off, a guy in a 4x4 Range Rover stopped alongside me and asked what I was doing. When I explained, he asked if he could donate £10! Again, the generosity of people astounded me. Here was a guy who drove past and stopped to donate money because he saw I was struggling to cycle.

When I eventually reached the café, I was shattered. Over a well-deserved lunch – and rest – I got chatting to another Land's End to John o' Groats guy. He had set off a few weeks earlier and was making a whole holiday out of it while also raising money for Macmillan. When he left the café, I told him I would try and catch him up – but added not to hold his breath!

Refuelled and rested, I set off for Wick. Not long after Berriedale, the A9 splits and you head onto the A99 coastal road with the cliffs in front of you. As I mentioned earlier, when you head towards Wick, it looks like the end of the world and you can see the top right hand of Scotland turning left. I kept thinking I was nearly there and that it must be closer than I'd thought. But if you look at the map of Scotland, just after Wick there is a part that sticks out into the North Sea and then returns back into Scotland. I had thought this was John o' Groats in the distance, but it wasn't. It reminded me of hill climbing, when you always think you are at the top but then you get over it and see another hill.

The worst of the cycling was over, though, and I had my head down and finally got some speed up. I was keen to catch up with my Macmillan cycling friend from the café if I could, and after a while I saw him in the distance. I'd made up my mind I wouldn't stop until I caught up with him, and when I did, we had a chat about the charity and why we were both challenging ourselves to raise money.

He explained that his wife had died a few months earlier, and his kids didn't stay near him. The Land's End to John o' Groats cycle was something he and his wife had wanted to do for years but had kept putting off for one reason or another. When they'd found out she had cancer, they'd made plans to make the trip, but then her illness took over and they hadn't managed. He said it was one of his biggest regrets that they hadn't done the cycle together. But he admitted that if she was still alive and well, they would probably have always made an excuse why they couldn't do it.

The advice he said he would give anyone was to capture the moments with those you love, and with those who love you. 'Never take them for granted, and do something nice for them every day, even if it is just holding a door open for them,' he told me.

I chatted to him a bit about Ian and we agreed that cancer is horrible, it has no conscience, it cares not a jot about people's plans or dreams, about how rich or poor people are or how fit and healthy they are, we both agreed we wished there could be a cure and families would not have to go through the heartache. We wished each other luck, then we parted and I headed off. I wanted to get the foot down as I was getting a good bit of energy from my lunch and wanted to finish as soon as possible. I was not really enjoying the last day's stretch and was desperate to just get finished and get back to my real life.

Wick was up ahead, and Gary was waiting to tell me that David had already reached my local bar in Spain. I looked on Facebook, and all day he had been taking the Mickey by posting pictures of him in the sun with a beer, or an ice cream in his hand, and asking if we had finished because he was getting so hot waiting.

We had also received a bid of £100 for Gary's bike, which was a good bit less than we'd hoped as it was worth £350, but Gary didn't seem too bothered.

I was told that Wick has the smallest street in the UK, (I didn't see it.) We had just 16 miles to go and my pace was slow, so I estimated only another 1 and a half hours of cycling to go. Gary was going to head up to John o' Groats, park the van, and cycle back until he reached me, then we would finish together.

For the next 6 or so miles, or maybe even more, I started to think back over the journey and how my time and life had changed in the last year.

I had discovered things about cancer that I would never wish on anyone; I had met some incredible people; I had opened my eyes to others, and seen how people react differently to cancer – how people avoid talking about it, and how people approach you about things.

In 2014, I lost my brother to cancer. A few weeks later my aunt & uncle died of cancer (Cousin John's mum and dad). My mum watched her sister die of cancer aged just 41, she watched my dad and also now her son.

We are not the only family to go through this, loads of families do. But until Ian died, I had never experienced the range of emotions which the families go through – the fears, the tears, the feeling of total helplessness.

As I cycled, I thought about the reason I was doing this challenge. It was easy to explain; it was to try and keep Ian alive as long as possible, to give him hope and something to focus on away from his illness, also Ian had asked me to do something for the nurses who he said 'had saved his life' so I was never going to say no.

The end of my journey was in sight. I had never been up here before, but I knew I was looking for the Journey's End signpost. It was a very eerie landscape; just like the end of the world. Looking out past Scotland, I could see all the Orkney Islands. Again, call me ignorant, but I'd had no idea they were all so close to the mainland.

It was a bit surreal seeing Gary up ahead, and I don't know if it was in my head, but the scenery suddenly became very atmospheric – like looking at a sepia photograph. He was waiting for me at the top of a hill, because he said he didn't want to come all the way down then have to cycle all the way back up. One thing Gary is not is lazy, but jokingly I might have called him something in colourful terms along those lines for not coming down to meet me.

As I got to the top, we then headed down the hill together, Gary shouted, 'C'mon, let's get some speed up and go for it!'

So we raced each other down into John o' Groats and he took me toward the sign, then he stopped so I could finish before him.

I pedalled up to the sign and touched it. I had just completed the Land's End to John o' Groats cycle and had beat Bullet Express. But, to be honest, there were no winners in this game.

22

'Being the first to cross the finish line makes you a winner in only one phase of your life. It's what you do after you cross the line that really counts.'

Ralph Boston, *retired American track athlete*

By the end of the cycle, the Macmillan fundraising page was sitting at just over £9000. And when we included all the cash donations and cheques, we reached our amazing target of £10,000.

It's now the 10th of June, 2015. Exactly one year from the day Ian died. I've been writing down my thoughts over the past year, at night, when alone, or when everyone is in bed – just little bits here and there. I enjoy looking back at memories and photos, and I just don't want to forget Ian. Hopefully, by writing this, we as a family will never forget.

Before Ian died, he requested I do a few things for him, and as time has passed, I've done exactly what he asked. From my point of view, I hope that the memory and the courage of my brother will always be remembered. As they say, 'No-one dies if they are remembered.'

When I started writing, I had no idea why I was doing it. But as my friend Andy said to me, 'Maybe the reason has still to come.'

As time has gone on, though, I now believe my reason is simple and is in the title.

I hope it's not just been a babble to anyone reading it.

Brother Allan, doing all Ian requested
00.05hrs
10th June, 2015

Part Three
Recovery, Acceptance, the End

23

"Gratitude unlocks the fullness of life, it turns what we have into enough. It turns denial into acceptance chaos into order, confusion to clarity. It can turn a meal into a feast, a house into a home and a stranger into a true friend."

Melody Beattie, *American author*

It's the 22nd of July, 2017, and I'm standing in the viewing gallery at the Stowe Circuit at Silverstone Racetrack in England, watching for a 12-year-old boy coming round the track on a Honda CRV 400cc racing motorbike.

Then I spot him. Every kid looks the same until you see their helmets, then you know who they are. The 12-year-old boy is my nephew, wee Sandy.

There is no rider for a fair distance in front of him, and no-one chasing up behind him. He is riding the 400cc bike effortlessly – not the fastest, but he was hitting apex to apex, like he was told to do. When he got to the straight part of track in front of me, he was tucking into the bike the way he had been told and opening the throttle right up. At the end of the straight, there were markers that had been shown to him and he was using them to come down the gears for braking before hitting the right to left-hand chicane. He came down the gears perfectly at each marker, got into the chicane, and away he would go with the throttle opened up again.

I watched him do this over and over again, and a tear came to my eye. I really wished Ian was there to witness this; I really wished my mate Andy Rankin was there to witness this.

I knew this could be Sandy's last ride on a racing motor-bike. As I watched him, I detected a maturity in Sandy that I had seldom seen. He was doing exactly what he had been told to do, 'Forget everyone else; it is not a race. Only you can control what you can do. Nothing you do can affect others, so just concentrate on yourself. Close everything out apart from your own ride, and just try your best.'

It hit me there and then that our recovery and acceptance was nearly complete.

When his session ended, I watched as he got helped off his bike at the pit lane garages, saw his rider bib number 036, and had a smile at the number as he disappeared into the garages. I then went into the waiting area beside all the other hopefuls' mums and dads, and waited on him coming out.

When Sandy emerged, he was beaming from ear to ear and as excited as I had seen him in a long time. I gave him a high five and a hug, and planted a big kiss on his head. He turned, punched me in the stomach, and laughed.

'Sandy, that's the best I have ever seen you on a motorbike, wee man.' I was just as excited as him but was trying not to show it. All we had to do now was to wait and see if Sandy had made the next cut of riders.

But whether he made the cut or not, was beside the point. Racing is not the be all and end all of our lives.

Our goal was dramatically different from the others in this racing game. And when I gave Sandy the high five and kiss, I knew our journey and recovery was nearing its end. I had turned a stranger into a true friend.

24

"If you have not resolved your grief, it will affect your future relationships including the one you have with yourself. Including the one you have with loved ones. It will keep us all in a holding pattern, putting a straitjacket on your love and chaining you to the past instead of moving you forward into the future."

Kate McGahan, *author and grief counsellor*

Ok, let me explain a little. I have fast-forwarded four years since Ian's death and my epic Land's End to John o' Groats charity cycle.

It is no secret that since Ian's death I have had to go through the grieving process. Grief is something that was new to me, and it's only now that I am starting to come to terms with how it works and how it affects people in similar situations.

Until I lost my brother, I had never heard of the 'Five stages of Grief'. They are:

DENIAL; ANGER; BARGAINING; DEPRESSION; and ACCEPTANCE.

When Ian was in hospital, I remember someone talking to me about the five stages of grief or five stages of death, so I Googled it, but it was all mumbo-jumbo to me. I never really paid any attention to it then, but without knowing it, I was probably starting my grief process and was in Denial.

What I have found to be true about the process is that although the five stages are labelled Denial, Anger, Bargaining, Depression, and Acceptance, they do not come in any particular order. I would say that's with one exception – and for me that would obviously be Acceptance.

I may be wrong, but Acceptance in my opinion over-rules the rest. If you have reached Acceptance, then in some way you have gained some sort of closure. I would always put Acceptance last on the list. It's a hard stage to reach, and I am sure many people never even actually get to this stage.

If I had to write my list in order, then I think it would read Anger, Denial, Depression, Bargaining, and – definitely last – Acceptance.

After Ian's death, I focused on the ride from Land's End to John o' Groats to raise as much money as possible for Macmillan Nurses and the Maggie's Centre at Monklands Hospital. But after the ride came a massive void, where life seemed to carry on for everyone else around me while mine seemed to just stop and I felt a huge void. Without knowing it, I was probably going through Depression. Looking back, I can see it more clearly now. From the outside, it probably looked like I was still carrying on with things and smiling, but inside I was screaming.

I wrote this poem not that long ago, and I tried to put across how I felt then.

5 Stages of Grief
You Are Never Alone

You hear the news that everyone fears,
Then comes the shock, the worry, and tears.
You feel like your life has been put on trial
But really, my friend, you're just in DENIAL.

So, after denial you just want to blame.
Our lives will now be never the same.
You struggle to breathe like being choked by a strangler,
You're starting to hate, but that's just the ANGER.

BARGAINING? With who? I look up to the sky
For guidance in God, as time flies me by.
Be better? Be wiser? And give something back?
Just something! Anything! Get your life back on track.

On the outside, you show you can laugh, joke, and smile,
But inside you're screaming; it's taking a while.
But with anger and blame, watch out for aggression,
Without you knowing, you're in a DEPRESSION.

ACCEPTANCE is the final chapter they teach.
The reality is, it's so hard to reach.
What's in our heads you can't buy steal or borrow.
Just sitting in silence and feeling the sorrow.

That's the stages, one through to five.
Remember the memories of loved ones gone by.
So, with these words I hope I have shown
There are others like you.
YOU ARE NEVER ALONE!

Strange thing is, until Ian died, I was never one for writing or reading books. But I needed to focus on something, and when I stayed up late at night unable to sleep, I just started writing down some things. And looking back at photos, I decided to write about the time from Ian first getting ill until my amazing bike ride.

I believe it was a kind of therapy to help me with undiagnosed depression, as I have since heard about people becoming creative after a loved one has died, or starting up charities. How many people get involved in charity work after a loved one has died? You see and hear about it all the time. It's all part of the Bargaining stage. People want to give something back. They see life differently and look through a different lens from others. If you meet someone who has suffered loss and is grieving, instantly you have that connection; you can almost immediately feel it just looking into their eyes.

In doing the bike ride, without even knowing it, I was probably going through the Bargaining stage, I wanted to do the ride and give as much back to the charities as possible. It doesn't just go away, though, and it's something now I can look back and understand.

When we initially planned the bike ride, the proceeds were to be given to the Macmillan Nurses and the Maggie's Centre at Monklands Hospital. We had arranged a meeting with Macmillan & Maggie's to let them know of the challenge and our intention to donate a 50/50 split of any money raised. But the Maggie's representative could not attend the meeting, and Macmillan seemed to take over by setting up a Go Fund me, online donate and text pages. So, the final amount of £10,000 raised by the cycle challenge was presented to Macmillan.

I spoke to David and Gary about it at the time, and we

promised that later in the year we would hold a dinner dance or do something else to raise money for Maggie's. We agreed that Maggie's would receive as much if not more than we'd raise from the bike ride.

I am pleased and proud to say that later that year I organised a Charity Race Night which raised just over £11,000, which was duly donated to The Maggie's Centre.

When Ian and Jean got married at the Maggie's Centre, it had not even officially been opened. So, it was nice to be invited to the grand opening by Scottish Professional Golfer Colin Montgomery a few weeks later.

This is a perfect example of what I mean about giving something back or going through the Bargaining stage. Professional Golfer Colin Montgomery created a drop-in centre to help cancer patients and families after the loss of his own mother.

I think anyone going through cancer treatment, or living with someone with a terminal illness, must experience Denial and at some point Anger. The Denial is obvious. All through Ian's illness, we were in Denial. You always think there will be a cure and that someone will say something at the last minute to save the day, but the reality is different. Even after Ian died, I was still in Denial and carried on as though he was still with us. As I mentioned earlier, I even picked up my phone to call him at one stage of the bike ride. I took young Sandy places and did as much as I could with him, but in the back of my mind I was always thinking it was temporary because Ian would be back shortly.

Anger and Blame need to be dealt with carefully. Without going into too much detail, during Ian's illness I looked at some people in the family in a purely negative way and I turned on a few of them during that time and immediately after the funeral. Without looking for excuses and in hindsight, I am sure Anger, Blame, and Depression all played a part in my actions and words at that time. It's something I massively regret, and even to this day it has not been resolved; I don't see it ever being resolved. That is just something I need to accept, but asking forgiveness from people who appear to have no empathy can lead down a road to emotional hell. And believe me when I say I have no time nor will to go down that road any more.

Filling the Void

Filling the void which is deep as it's wide
is just so hard with no Ian by my side.
A walking contradiction that we all knew,
His team were the famous
Red, white, and blue.
We travelled all over,
North, South, East and West
taking the piss but was always in jest.
From Larkhall to Moscow, New York to the Keys,
No-one could stop us,
We just did as we pleased.
Time is a healer;
Is it? I ask.
So far, I'd say no,
as I stick to the task.
So forget me not, that's what Ian would say.
No, Ian, I won't,
you are with me today.
No matter what's said
Or how hard that I hide,
The void is still deep
Just as it is wide!!

Once the dust had settled after Ian died, we decided as a family that Sandy should continue with his Mini Moto GP racing. It was something Ian started with him before he died, but unfortunately never got to see him compete. During the winter, we got sponsorship from Bullet Express and Sandy began practising for the next season starting in March. Ian had bought Sandy a good little race bike which was able to compete up front with the other riders.

Andy Rankin, me, and a friend of my wife's, Carmino Martucci, travelled all over the UK in Ian's old van. Like Ian before us, we would grab some boil-in-a-bag food, some Pot Noodles, chocolate bars, and a case of beer most weekends, and travel with Sandy to go-kart tracks up and down the country.

The very first race we took Sandy to down near Northampton, he won. And he continued winning here and there all season.

On the final day of his first season in the Mini Moto GP British Championship, he was beaten into a very creditable 3rd place overall.

During this time, I also got Sandy interested in football and I took him to as many games as I could. On one occasion, one of his race weekends was down near Dover, so Andy and I borrowed his passport from Jean and took him across to France to watch one of the Euro Championship games in Lille.

On the 18th April, 2015, I took Sandy up to the Isle of Skye. It was exactly one year after I'd made the same trip with Ian. This time, I got a big oak cross made and engraved with Ian's name running from top to bottom and 'Carrying out your wishes' from left to right. My intention was to lay it somewhere on the route on the way up to the Inaccessible Pinnacle.

It had always been my intention to take Sandy along, so I had taken him climbing a few times beforehand, and had even let him try a few climbing walls to get him prepared.

The bizarre thing was that Sandy wanted to carry the cross, and he was determined to carry it all the way to the 'Inaccessible Pinnacle', despite the fact that it was almost the same size as him. I also got him a Climbers against Cancer T-shirt which he wore under his dad's hoodie – the one Ian wore when he climbed it in 2014.

Like his dad the year before, I could not believe how determined the little guy was, and eventually we made it to the 'Inaccessible Pinnacle'. Once there, he was determined to climb it, and let me help him abseil off it.

We dug the cross firmly and deeply into the ground on a ridge just off the main route. I concreted it all in, and it still remains there to this day. I've been up a few times since, and I always take some oil and a brush to treat it. I really hope it stays 'Steadfast and Sure' up there for many years.

Bullet Express, along with a few others, helped to sponsor Sandy for the next season's Mini Moto GP Championship and, with help from his mum Jean, we got him two new race bikes to ride in two different classes – Air-Cooled, and Water-Cooled.

Again, Andy and Carmino travelled up and down the UK in the van with us, and we had loads of ups and downs and cheers and tears. But on the last day of the 2016 Championship Season, Sandy managed to win in both the Water-Cooled and Air-Cooled classes, making him a Double British Mini Moto GP Champion!

Without Sandy's knowledge, we had taken along the Union Jack that had covered Ian's coffin, and we draped it over the fence at one of the corners so that every lap Sandy passed there was a little bit of his dad watching him.

The three of us were extremely proud of Sandy's achievement, and I was really touched when he let me keep his British Championship Trophies, which I proudly display and see each day in my office.

For the following season, Sandy was picked to be part of British Superbike Team Tyco BMW, in the British Fab Racing Championship, which meant moving up onto a bigger bike class while still racing his Mini Moto GP Bikes. The season began with us doing winter testing in Cartagena in Murcia, Spain, and then travelling up to take part in a winter testing championship in Finestrat, Alicante.

On his first race weekend in the bigger bike class, Sandy made it onto the podium in third place.

We found the third season much more demanding, though, both financially and with time spent away from family.

But Sandy got a few more race wins under his belt, and was selected to be part of the British Talent Cup Selection process to be held at Silverstone Race Circuit. This new competition was billed as being an opportunity for young British riders to mix with some of the best racers in the world and to be a stepping stone to the international stage.

He had also been invited to enter a race at the Donnington 500 race weekend, which would be Sandy's first race on his big bike at a world-famous track.

Without his knowledge, we had decided that Sandy would only race the following season if he got picked for the British Talent Cup. We were aware that being involved at that level brought so many more challenges: the competitiveness is so much fiercer; the finance is through the roof; and you need a full-time mechanic. Turning up with boil-in-a-bag food and cases of beer would not cut it any more.

We knew we would be out of our depth. Ian was the brother who was mechanically-minded and I am pretty sure that if he was still with us, Sandy would do so much better on his bike journey. Nevertheless, Sandy had taken us on an incredible journey from practising a Mini Moto in a factory car park in Glasgow, to winning the British Championship, to rubbing shoulders with some of the best motorbike riders in the world.

The Donnington 500 race was a perfect example of how out of our depth we were. We could not get his bike working properly, and by the time qualifying came round, Sandy only made it to the first corner before his bike broke down. It meant he would have to start from the back of the grid in 16th position.

There were three races which, depending on your lap times, would move you up the grid. We eventually got his bike working, or at least ready to participate, and by the third race Sandy actually led going into the first corner.

But that was just the way it was with us and Sandy that season. He's the only kid I know that could start from the back of a race grid at the beginning of the day, and lead at the front by the end of the day.

That then took us to Silverstone racetrack for the British Talent Cup. There were 90 UK riders chosen from 220 entries to be given a chance of a place in the British Talent Cup Team. The organisers were looking for 25 of the best riders with the potential to possibly take a step towards racing Moto GP. Alberto Puig, a former GP motorcycle road racer and Honda manager, was given the task of picking the best riders.

Andy could not make the trial at Silverstone due to work commitments, so this turned out to be one of the few occasions when Sandy and I were flying solo. We had already looked at the finances for the following year and predicted it would cost approximately £15,000-£20,000 for Sandy to compete the following season. Between us, we knew that it would have to end. The British Talent Cup would be Sandy's last hope, as it gave kids a real chance with Honda and the British Talent Cup picking up the cost for everything.

Sandy rode his heart out. He was jumping from the equivalent of 125cc onto a 400cc, and the bike looked huge on him. But to be fair, he handled it well.

It was without doubt one of my proudest days racing with Sandy, and I really wished Ian and Andy had been there to witness it.

Looking around at some of the young riders' parents, who had become great friends in this journey, it was obvious that some had put their life into this racing. There are a few who can afford it, but most are living from hand to mouth, sleeping in vans week after week, hoping that one day their kid will be next Valentino Rossi.

To be honest, I felt a bit of a fraud. Sandy had a great chance of going on in the sport, but I knew that if he failed we had plenty of other things to fall back on.

In the end, Sandy got cut when it went down to the last 50 riders. There were no big tears, like some of the kids, or furious tantrums from dads when their kids got pulled from the selection.

There was just an honest realisation from Sandy. The motorbike journey and that chapter in our lives were at an end. It had been fun while it lasted. We met some beautiful people along the way but our time in the sport was at an end.

Motorbiking and go karting had been Ian's life and a big part of Sandy's life, but it was not mine. There is so much more in this life that I want to show him.

But I will be forever grateful to Sandy. He helped me probably more than I helped him, and more than he or anyone will ever know. By focusing on his racing, I worked through my personal stages of grief.

My mate Andy has been my own personal psychologist for the past four or five years, and I will always be in his debt. We have driven all over the UK together, weekend after weekend, and he's listened to story after story. How he has put up with us, God only knows. But as long as Andy is here, I know I am never alone.

As a family, we are getting on with things without Ian. Life will never be the same, but I love watching Sandy trying new things; he is so like Ian it's frightening. He has now moved on to snowboarding, along with me, Andy, and my daughter Sacha. And he still comes to the football and on the odd climb with me.

On the 18th of April, 2017, I went back up to the Isle of Skye to mark what would have been Ian's 50th Birthday.

Happy Birthday, big bruv,
Hope your smiling from up there above.
50 years old you would have turned today,
If that horrible disease hadn't taken you away.
When I look back upon our years,
It's hard to see beyond the tears.
Remember as a kid, I was no more than 8?
You showed me the world beyond the gate,
and Mum just shouted,
'Don't bring him back late!'
In our teens, remember bunking off school?
You took me with you to fish, shoot, and climb,
we were just two kids at the start of our prime.

In our 20s working together we did,
albeit far away,
North Sea on the rigs.
30s now, we were getting on a bit,
supposed to grow up.
We thought, 'F&@k that shit!'
You started your business around that time,
I watched in awe as it started to shine.
40s now, and we had kids all around,
Dillon, Alex, Sara, Sacha, and Sandy were found.
I laughed as I heard you were going to be Papa,
but you were the one who thought it amazing.
Changing the nappies for grandkid, wee Mason.
I'm so sorry, Ian, no 50s' tales to tell;
47 was the year that you fell.
So today I'll sit and have a beer,
And keep watch over the family, they are all quite near.
I wonder what we would be doing today.
I just pray that we will be back together some day.
18th of April, Happy Birthday, big bruv,
From all down here, we send you our love.

As time moves on, there are loads of things I still want to do with Ian's lads. We are all quite close now, probably closer than we would ever be if Ian was still here, but there is something I will enjoy watching as I grow old. When I look back to when Ian was diagnosed as terminal, one of his final wishes was to catch another salmon in the River Lochy. Cancer never gave him that wish. That's the thing about cancer: it just does not care about people's wishes or dreams.

As Ian used to say, 'Man plans and God laughs.' But mark my words, there is a salmon in that River Lochy with Ian's name on it, and believe me when I say that one of his lads will catch it.

And I'll be lying back on the riverbank smiling.

So, let's go way back to the start of our story, when I got the call about Ian while I was watching Glasgow Rangers in a Challenge Cup game in Division 3. Our team has since worked its way back up the leagues through blood, sweat, and tears, and is now sitting proudly at the correct end of the Scottish Premier League table.

'No-one Dies If They Are Remembered.'

"No one dies if they are   Remembered"

Can you see this cross up here, brother of mine?
Where we once came to walk, laugh and climb.
Great laughs and jokes along the way
Five years ago this very day.

How you managed I'll never know
Fast, Determined, Brave and Bold
The news not wanted had just been told
The fear of you not seeing old.

We sang "The train it keeps a rolling"
We even sang "Walk the line"
Johnny Cash still gets me Bruv
Every single time.

Remember us watching the sea that day
As the waves crashed to the shore
The waves don't crash as often now
But each time they're still as sore.

So whether its a bright, Spring April day
Or a cold, day in December
Remember this, I'll say it again
"No one dies if they are   Remembered."

Lightning Source UK Ltd.
Milton Keynes UK
UKHW020631301019
352506UK00007B/44/P

9 781916 238107